Keep the faith
David

The fading doctrines of Jesus Christ

by Rt Revd Dr. David E Carr
OBE OSL EKHC

CELUIC
BREEZE
PUBLISHING

Published by
Celtic Breeze Publishing
The Warehouse44
44 Oxford Street
Leamington Spa
United Kingdom
CV32 4RA

www.orderofstleonard.org

The fading doctrines of Jesus Christ

First edition

ISBN: 978-1-5272-8095-3

A catalogue record of this book is available from the British Library

Published by Celtic Breeze Publishing, an imprint of The Order of St Leonard.

For more information, please email: admin@orderofstleonard.org

Published in Great Britain

The fading doctrines of Jesus Christ

by Rt. Rev'd Dr. David E Carr OBE OSL EKHC

My great desire is to see the Christian Church retain its cutting edge in a provocative generation. The basic theological teachings delivered by Jesus Christ have, in many Churches, been relegated to the historic. This book seeks to refocus the Church on its mandate to deliver the gospel – as Jesus preached it.

My reflection on the doctrines and theological premise of the Christian faith have been greatly enhanced by the added research provided by Mandy Cooper. Mandy completed this valued task while studying at Harvard University. Thank you, Mandy, for your love and commitment. Both Mandy and her husband Revd Canon Dave Cooper have, over many years, been incredibly supportive to me personally, and to the Order of St Leonard.

As this book goes to print, we are many months into the pandemic that has swept the world. No one has escaped its impact – whether in terms of health, emotional wellbeing or economy. Our lives have been changed beyond measure – and in this time of separation, we need to focus ever more on the things that unify us. We need to focus on Christ.

Rt. Revd Dr. David E Carr OBE OSL EKHC
Solihull, United Kingdom
November 2020.

Introduction

This book has been difficult, to write. Why? It's not easy when you see what appears to be a subtle decline in theological and biblical authenticity.

I've called it 'The Fading Doctrines of Jesus Christ', simply because many of the foundational teachings of the faith have been either simplified to the extent of trivia, or completely replaced by what l call 'situation and issue theology'.

What do l mean?

Having been a motivational speaker in the insurance industry l fully appreciate the power of positive thinking; yet is positive thinking always spiritual thinking? l hear sermons that attract crowds causing the people to go out on a high, yet not quite challenged by the Holy Spirit.

These sermons major on processes to achieve certain goals and aspirations in life. Issues in family, business and finance are all good subjects for discussion but are not based on the fundamentals of true faith.

Conviction of the Holy Spirit is deemed an historic concept. Discipleship seems more of a buzzword than a reality; the gospel being designed to deliver a message according to the culture receiving it, adapting itself as an answer to the contemporary needs and wants of the seeker, not as an expression of the truth of scripture. Truth is truth; and while some truths may be difficult to hear, we cannot simply deny those which are challenging, unpopular or that contradict the lifestyle of the believer. Scripture is not to be edited, adapted, modified – the Word itself even cautions against such attempts.

I'm simply a pastor who truly believes in the fundamental truths of the Christian faith and what Jesus preached.

What did the Apostles preach? What did the early church fathers preach? Are we still preaching it? These are the questions I wish to ask in this book. Beyond this, if we are not preaching this way, then why is this the case? What do we hope to achieve?

As I enter my fifth decade of pastoral ministry, I reflect on the last sixty years of Christian doctrine and teachings that I have either sat beneath or delivered myself.

I would be seen by most to be of the Evangelical/Pentecostal tradition by upbringing; however, my influence theologically takes into account much of the early church fathers.

I would see beauty in most of the theological traditions including Wesleyan, Anglican and Celtic spirituality. Having served the Pentecostal streams for nearly thirty years as a pastor and leader, I realised that my personal and my church's theology was truly Pentecostal more than Pentecostalist.

The first is a Holy Spirit experience, the second a denominational expression. That, of course, is in no way a rebuff of them; I have loved both Elim and Assemblies of God, as well as the two New Testament Churches and have either served or ministered in all of them for over fifty years. But I have needed to embrace a wider culture than any one of these lovely people can individually offer.

As Founding Pastor of Renewal Christian Centre, we are part of the Free Methodist Church. We do, however, attract people from many denominations, who bring with them a synergy and freshness to all we are and do.

As a Church, and as a leader, we have never needed to seek an identity in following outpouring or trends or teachings of other significant Churches. This is not in any way a superior attitude, but simply we have heard what the Spirit has been saying to the Church. He can create a defined national, or international, outpouring without making every church a clone of one another.

Theology can seem lifeless; it is however the depth of our spiritual foundations. In my early life l submitted to my brother Michael's teaching as my Pastor. The magnitude and depth of his teaching was transforming. This isn't nepotism. We haven't always agreed on everything! But his understanding of scripture was profound and I would sit, every Sunday and Tuesday, under that richness for eighteen years.

To be truthful, it was so deep and eloquent that I could seldom tell you, either during the service or after the service, what he had said! Yet when I was filled with the Holy Spirit it all became understandable and relevant. The Holy Spirit brings back to memory that which we have already absorbed.

You need to learn it, so that He can use your learning as kindling for His fire. Without this, we can of course experience Him, but our study gives us greater insight and revelation in context. Those eighteen years, together with the five needed to be ordained, gave me over twenty-three years of bible knowledge with which to begin my ministry journey. And the study has never ceased, the learning does not stop. Anyone who loves scripture will understand its unique quality for the layering of messages, allegories and analogy – the more we study, the deeper we go into the true meaning of the Word.

As Preachers who know Christ, we ask the question: as good and effective as our preaching may be, what ratio of sermons do we deliver that actually speak of Christ and Him crucified?

Many fine Preachers today preach many a dynamic series; however, they are often derived from business principles creating a motivational climax. I know; I travelled internationally delivering such secular seminars for the insurance industry.

There is nothing wrong with a positive, goal-setting lifestyle that is the product of true discipleship. The problem is, do we see it as the power of positive thinking, or do we properly acknowledge that our life is subject to the power of Christ crucified?

The Apostle Paul, who was the greatest contributor to the New Testament, unashamedly said,

"l preach Christ and Him Crucified."

Yet in saying that, he appreciated that it would only be partially acceptable to his audiences.

To the Jews, it was offensive; to Gentiles, it's all foolishness, but to those who are being saved, it's the power of God unto Salvation (an ongoing process).

The Tablet, the official magazine of the Roman Catholic Church (dated 1928) said:

"It follows that if the Cross, the hated Cross, had not been an essential part of the Good News which Paul had to tell, he would have glossed it over - explained it away. Paul saw clearly that this Cross was a brake on his wheel. Writing to a group of converts whom he had made in Corinth, he summed up the difficulty in one of those thoroughly Pauline sayings which hit the mark like polished stone."

In our quest to preach the cross and the effect that Jesus had on humanity, we can so easily excuse ourselves from who Jesus is, what His ministry was and the impact of His teaching.

I was sitting up in bed one morning in Australia, waiting for the family that I was staying with to rise, when I felt a compulsion to flick through the New Testament. I believe that I heard the Holy Spirit say to me, "Read the words of Jesus...the red bits"

With the day dawning I read the book of Matthew, just the red bits, and that day changed my understanding of who He was and what He taught. I realised that, as a preacher, I seldom preached His words, His teachings or His theology. From that trip onwards, I changed all my sermons and saw incredible things happen.

The Christian Church, throughout history, has often compromised essential truth to argue over preferred truth; essential truth would be the need and ability to find forgiveness for sin, the understanding of personal holiness, sanctification, justification, righteousness, love and peace, the need for baptism in water and usage of both the fruit and gifts of the Holy Spirit.

We need a rethink of what it means to be truly 'born again'.

But the preaching of this preferred truth, the liturgy of the church, dress code, the style of the Communion and worship is preached at the expense of the reality of essential truth; we argue Calvinism or Arminianism, as if the other view was unacceptable for salvation.

I appreciate that, to some, these subjects are deeply challenging however it would be true to say that out of the estimated thirty-three thousand denominations, streams and groupings in the world, most are separated by preferred truth rather than essential truth.

All this negates the importance of the call of Jesus during His passion prayer to the Father in John 17. It's for a "Oneness", and oneness exceeds unity. It's a merging of thought and heart.

This Oneness was modelled by both the Father and the Son, you could see the love and trust that they had for each other. Yet Jesus desired for this same "oneness" to be available to us "that they may be one as we are one". In our case, one in purpose and spirit not in substance.

It would be true to say that every generation has tried to apply the gospel in differing ways; ways designed to help the non-Christian more fully understand the message of the gospel.

It must also be noted that, in the desire to accommodate the changing cultural needs of society, the message can either be distorted or even lost. This was the classic condition during the Wesleyan Revival. The Church had compromised its message and deteriorated into compromise and even corruption. The Wesleys preached repentance from sin, the need to offer up a totally surrendered life through the conviction of sin, holiness. Historians have said that this Revival may even have saved the nation from a French style revolution.

Charles Wesley, also an accomplished preacher, composed an estimated eight thousand hymns. Why? For those who couldn't read, it was theology to music!

The need was, firstly, for salvation, followed by discipleship. The worship of the day was scripture, a modern Psalm. I love so much of modern worship, yet a lot of it lacks any theological credibility. To those who have never picked up a bible, the song needs to lead them there.

General William Booth of the Salvation Army held that worship music was a tool for salvation. He issued guidelines to bandsmen and songsters to produce simple songs with an emphasis on a strong, clear, 'soul-saving' message. He also believed Salvationists 'must sing good tunes' and didn't care much whether you call it secular or sacred. He said, "I rather enjoy robbing the devil of some of his choicest tunes". They believe that in today's mixed congregations, the music must be broad in its ability to reach all ages and cultures – but the theological message must be sound. The style and tone of the music can, of course, be written to appeal to any audience – but the meaning and the message must be theologically sound. Inculcating motivational messages into worship songs may support popularity, but it rather misses the point. Worship leaders and musicians should be guided more by the theologians – whether by spoken word, written word or sung word, our theology must remain true.

Music is often the first experience of a new visitor to church. To welcome the stranger into the life of the kingdom is of immense importance, however we must never negate the very reason that the Holy Spirit came. If we are positioning our worship so prominently – up front and centre of our preaching and connection with the people – then it must be challenged in the same way as our preaching – it cannot confuse or obfuscate the message of the bible.

To convict the world of Sin, Righteousness and the judgment to come.

(John 16:8 ESV)

Sin. Righteousness. Judgment. It might appear that all three of these expressions could seem negative, condemning, or restrictive. It might not appeal to the contemporary church-going audience. But it's the only way humanity can find solace and forgiveness from our fallen state.

My deep concern that caused me to write this book is the apparent lack of conviction seen amongst those entering and leaving our churches today. I am concerned that in the drive to bring people in – and to keep them coming back – the church has modified itself to suit the seeker. But this is the opposite of what should be happening. Churches are failing in their duty – their biblical duty, the instruction of Christ – to challenge the people and to preach the gospel, undiluted, unaltered and unapologetically.

To convict means to reprove, admonish and to tell a fault. How comfortable is the church today in delivering messages of approval or admonishment? So, as we look at the biblical tenets of stability needed for a secure Christian life, l trust you see the need for a positive analysis of our present stance and a willingness to make any adjustment needed for a biblical faith of endurance.

We shouldn't be afraid to preach truth. It may offend some people. They may not come back. They may not pat us on the back and tell us what a wonderful sermon it was. They may complain about us to their friends. But are we called to tell people what they want to hear? Or are we called to preach the truth. I think the answer to that is straightforward, but incredibly complex in its understanding and application in a church that is compelled by its need to grow and its desire to keep people coming back.

As I grow older, I see that a true Christian life may have started with what was called a 'sinner's prayer' however, searching the scriptures I'm convinced that discipleship is to last the lifetime of the believer; it produces the fruit of the Spirit which is the mark of true salvation. It's not enough for a new believer to pray the prayer and then look at what the church can do for them. It's not enough to keep coming back to listen to an encouraging word in a warm room with a hot drink and a chance to chat with your friends. All those things are pleasant, but they aren't the reason. My concern is that the side-effects of a contemporary welcome become the confluence of influence. Now that churches appear on 'Trip Advisor' and are 'rated' for their visitor experience, this heralds the decline into comparison sites for local churches – where people compare the quality of the coffee and ease of parking as reasons to attend.

So, I turn to the story of the sower, in which we find the key to all the parables. Jesus openly said, "If you don't understand this one, you won't understand any of them".

Jesus never spoke of backsliders in this parable. He spoke of four responses to the gospel message, but only one produced the fruit.

Jesus said that there was one main parable that unless it was understood, no other could be correctly interpreted. That was the one of the sower in Matthew 13

This story is simple yet deeply concerning, it speaks of four reactions to the gospel of Jesus Christ – the places where the seeds fell determining the outcome.

Hard Ground

Those who are resistant to the Word of God are hardened to the things of truth, should an opportunity occur, triviality takes away the very thoughts of true repentance.

Rocky Ground

Those who have received an emotional or intellectual experience, no depth of reality, flourish for a time, yet when difficult times come, there is no foundational substance to draw on, they fall away.

Thorny Ground

Those who maintain their previous life full of this world's cares and suppressive ways; There are people who have problems, and there are problem people, because their Christian commitment didn't reach the soul...their personality has not been freed from the daily troubles, they then begin to choke the very life out of them.

Good Ground

Those who open themselves up to the Holy Spirit mind, body, soul, spirit...the evidence of this is fruit as seen in Galatians 5. The quality is constant, but the growth is related to ability 30, 60, 100-fold.

Churches understand the need for good soil – but the challenge is in tending the seeds long enough for them to establish roots. I understand the reason for the seeker friendly gospel. I understand why churches strive for comfort and relevance in the contemporary world. It's difficult – I'm not denying that. But you can't switch the ground mid-course. If people stay for the side-shows, the minute you switch to truth, they'll leave anyway. The message here is clear – start with the good ground, stay with the good ground.

This book is not an easy read.

It was born out of a concern that the global Church in the west is facing a challenge. We need to look at what it is we are preaching and modelling to people. Are we seeing genuine repentance, conversion, or disciples being formed? Yes, in some cases, however, there seems to be a growing philosophy in marketing a message of a motivational lifestyle. It is subtle in its presentation and wears the cloak of scriptural authenticity, yet it is seldom birthed in fundamental doctrines.

The basics of faith experienced throughout generations has, in many cases, been replaced by a presentation of goal setting; the feel good, motivational lifestyle. I trust I've not been pessimistic about the Church's future! I believe in modern presentation. We live in a challenging post-Christian age in many countries of the western world. It's not the presentation of dark auditoriums, smoke machines, flashing lights and torn jeans - l can live with that at the age of 75.

But what we cannot permit or tolerate is the often-compromised, light-weight message that sees little conviction, leading to little conversion. We are not performers; we are a royal priesthood. We are not there to build reputation, experience and events. As we decrease, He increases.

Simply, we need to teach this generation the stability of His word and the power of His Holy Spirit. We need leaders who are so immersed and absorbed within the word that they would be unable to speak otherwise. We need to be consistent in this truth – so that regardless of church attended, the people hear the same truth, the same gospel from the same Jesus.

I want to thank all those over the years that didn't dilute the word when trying to teach me the importance of the "Jesus Doctrine". It has given me a passion that has not diminished during 48 years of pastoral ministry.

I mentioned being challenged some years ago to read the 'red bits' - just the words of Jesus. It transformed my thinking and theological perspective and I invite and challenge you to do the same.

Like the Apostle Paul, we are called to preach Christ and Him crucified. This book is intended as not just a challenge, but as an encouragement to the new generations of pastors, leaders and believers to stick to the truth and the truth will set you free. Always. This book has been completed in my new role as Founding Pastor. Yes, my days as Senior Pastor have ended and it's time to let the younger visionaries go for God. I will still be preaching, teaching and writing, as well as overseeing the Order of St Leonard and Chaplaincy both for the NHS and training Chaplains for the community throughout the UK.

Age doesn't diminish passion...it just weakens the legs!

See you in the next book!

David
Rt Revd Dr David Carr OBE OSL EKHC

SIN

As we look at the three things that the Holy Spirit came to convict us of, let's first look at the definition of sin:

SIN: An immoral act considered to be a transgression against divine law; to commit an offence. In simple terms, it means we have broken or are breaking God's law.

This conviction, rather than humiliating the individual, brings home the need and the provision for a fallen humanity to embrace the righteousness of Christ. The explanation of sin is to be considered useful and helpful – just like the laws of statute that give instruction on behaviour, it gives instruction and boundaries to right-thought.

Romans 3:23 declares that we have all committed the offence of sin and fallen short of the glory of God. We have offended God by a self-determined will of self-gratification. Frank Sinatra would no doubt agree that we "did it our way ".

Sin is not so much what we do before God or man, but who we are before God and man.

When we stand before Almighty God the first question will be, "who are you"? Not, "what have you done?" We are not a shopping list of actions and deeds – the world takes care of those for us. Our relationship with Christ determines the thought – the predeterminate to action. If we were all living in righteousness, under God's law, in truth and in Spirit – then maybe the laws of man would be redundant.

The difference is that humanity – the humanist view of society – doesn't much care for how you think. There is no law or punishment against thought – no matter how dark or evil. The law looks at action – or attempts/planning at action (the preparation) – but not at the thoughts which predicated such.

This relationship, who we are in Christ, is of greater importance than what we have done for Him, even though that is of immense importance. Preachers must not play down the seriousness of sin and its consequences to the human soul. Sin came by the ability of humanity to choose between dependence on God, or total independence from God. When the relationship between God and the individual is in righteousness, there is no need to negotiate with the world. There is no need to feel admonished by the pastor for wrong thoughts or actions – because such would simply never cross the mind. The church is not designed to intervene in this relationship–it's designed to help it to grow, to elicit understanding, to demonstrate the relationship in action, to support the world-livers in their transition to a state of righteousness in God. Here, is the place of serenity – of casting cares upon Him; of trusting Him and His word. This transcends the church and people relationship completely. And yet, Jesus told us to fellowship with one another.

Why might this be?

We are a people of creativity and stories. The parables of Jesus demonstrate that the way to learning is analogous and practiced, experientially delivered and utilising every aspect of our minds – critical thinking, imagination, memory and emotion. These experiences of church are the lived stories of today – the live-action demonstration of a people sold-out for Christ. Sociology compels communities (of every kind) to be as one, to keep one another on the agreed path of behaviour. So, too, does connection with the community of the church. When we don't understand or are pulled by the world – the fellowship around us gives us strength as we find our way back to Him – to the teaching of the word. This is why the teaching of the church cannot emulate the world – it's too confusing. In trying to be 'like' the world (to 'relate' to people) it can represent itself as being the 'same' as the world – which is entirely the wrong message.

I taught a group of young people some years ago. And, like many young Christians, they were struggling with the concept of physical relationships and what they 'were and were not allowed to do' as Christian youth before marriage, attempting to seek sanction and 'permission'.

My answer was very simple. I used an analogy and said;

'Imagine you are driving your car upwards along a mountain road. The road is not fenced to the left side, with a sheer drop over it that increases the further you progress. Over the sheer drop is certain death. To the right side, looms the comfort of the sheer rock face of the mountain, guarding your path.

Now, back to your original question. Ask me how close to the left hand edge it's OK to drive?'

Genesis 3:1

Genesis provides us with the first description in scripture of what is called sin, the action displayed by Eve and then later Adam reveals the desire of the human heart to divorce itself from spiritual dependency or accountability to God. The sin is predicated by the thought – the desire that overwhelmed and created disobedience to God's instruction. This resulted in man's inability to maintain the expected mark of righteousness that allowed humanity to walk with God in the cool of the day.

Bakers Evangelical dictionary of Bible Theology tells us: "We see the tendency of sin to begin with a subtle appeal to something attractive and good in itself, to an act that is somehow plausible and directed toward some good end. Throughout the bible, almost every sin reaches for things with some intrinsic value such as security, knowledge, peace, pleasure or a good name. But behind the appeal to something good, sin ultimately involves a raw confrontation between obedience and rebellion"

In that independence they did physically walk away from God – the scripture notes that He came looking for them! They no longer turned up for the daily walk in the cool of the day. But love endures and is seen in the action of God looking for them. The relationship from man to God had died – man was now dead in trespasses and sin.

Even the righteousness of God, through faith in Jesus Christ, to all and on all who believe. For there is no difference; for all have sinned and fall short of the glory of God, being justified freely by His grace through the redemption that is in Christ Jesus, whom God set forth as a propitiation by His blood, through faith, to demonstrate His righteousness, because in His forbearance God had passed over the sins that were previously committed, to demonstrate at the present time His righteousness, that He might be just and the justifier of the one who has faith in Jesus.
(Romans 3:22-26 NKJV)

The lack of teaching on this subject has caused many to refer to sin as problems, issues and circumstances - we must therefore consider the consequences of not revealing this deadly condition.

This descriptive word of 'sin' is often described in this way, 'remove the S and the N and you are left with the I'. It's this 'I' factor that causes the relational issues. The remedy? The cross; it's simply the 'I' crossed out!

Sin has universal applications, as we have seen in Romans. if all have sinned, then Christ - if he loved the world - must die for all. As we have seen, The Holy Spirit comes to convict (reveal) to all – to everyone - that we have fallen well below the standard required by a Holy God.

So, sin is not just actions, it is attitude. Sin towards God is one of attitude – of thought. We are sinners before Christ, yet we can sin not just against God but also against our fellow humanity.

Only Christ can reconcile humanity to God.

There is one God and one Mediator who can reconcile God and humanity—the man Christ Jesus.

(1 Timothy 2:5 NLT)

We, however, can, should and must forgive those who 'trespass against us'. Else we are not in rightness of thought. It's those who have been reconciled to the Father who can and must reconcile between each other.

When we who have sinned against God find full forgiveness, then the expectation is that we are also to forgive. If not, we are called 'wretched'.

Few churches seem willing, through social fear, to preach that humanity is enslaved in sin. If a doctor describes a malignant tumour as a cyst, they are not lessening the prognosis, they are simply lying about the diagnosis. Doctors are trusted to tell the truth – it is absolutely expected of them to outline the scenario as they see it before them. People may cry and plead against the diagnosis, it may be uncomfortable and even distressing for the physician to break the news to them – but they are ethically and professionally bound to the truth. If a human profession can do this – and be expected to do this – then why not the church, with its spiritual imperative to preach the gospel? A doctor does not water or dilute the truth. A doctor is not fearful that the patient will leave the hospital and never return. This may be the case and the patient may reject the diagnosis and go in search of a second opinion – but this does not sway the doctor's delivery of the news. In fact, a doctor providing minimal or inaccurate accounts of disease would be avoided by patients – not sought out for providing the 'preferred response'. Dr Luke repeats the words of Jesus, "I must preach the Good News of the Kingdom of God...because that is why I was sent." (Luke 4:43 NLT). All doctors understand that truth is absolute. It's time for the church to understand this, too – no matter how unpopular the diagnosis might be.

When we compromise our preaching so that the public who venture into our meetings go out seeking treatment for a cyst rather than a tumour, then the relief they seek is short lived.

The Apostle Paul, fully understanding that the preaching of the Cross is about sin, death, judgment, reconciliation and newness of life, admits that to the religious, it's offensive. Religious people do not want to be told that they are living in a self-induced system that attempts to justify themselves, their religious actions, or self-effort. They seldom feel easy being identified as a sinner! To the intellectual and the humanist, Paul confesses that many see the preaching of the cross as embarrassing and beyond logic.

But Paul's experience is that those who are open to such teaching experience a spiritual power that saves them, cleanses them, re-births them from the consequences of sin - those who are being saved from the consequences of sin. He calls the preaching of the cross, "the power of God unto salvation". So sin is the inability to comply with the demands of God's righteousness.

We can, and must, be conscious of the reason for the bloody carnage of the cross – blood, sweat and tears; this Christian faith is not synthetic, it's sacrificial. If the Church is to maintain its authenticity in the twenty-first century, it must maintain its original theology and lifestyle.

Sin is not a descriptor for 'fun' in a promiscuous society; it's the biggest killer of the human race!

RIGHTEOUSNESS

Righteousness. Just or innocent-equality of character. The opportunity to be reconciled with God, so negating the damaging qualities of sin. To preach righteousness is to bring people into a right relationship with the Almighty. It's God's gift of a corrective authority that enables one to think and live according to the precepts of God. Righteousness is acknowledgment of the law of God completed in Christ. Simply, He is all that is right, so in Him is all righteousness.

Whoever purses righteousness and love finds life, prosperity and honour.

(Proverbs 21:21 NIV)

Righteousness is not adopting a monastic attitude to life, but rather being inspired to live motivated by the Holy Spirit and grounded in His Word. Put simply, this about exchanging my negativity, which leads to death, for His positivity which leads to life, For the soul that sins will die (Ezekiel 18:20 ESV), however the gift of God is eternal life through Jesus Christ, our Lord.

The Holy Spirit deliberately sandwiches righteousness between sin and judgment, so offering humanity the opportunity to avoid the consequences of a sinful life. Righteousness brings freedom and deliverance, it's the preservation of God's grace. His favour saved us, His righteousness sustains us.

For the grace of God has appeared that offers salvation to all people. It teaches us to say "No" to ungodliness and worldly passions, and to live self-controlled, upright and Godly lives in this present age. (Titus 2:11-12 NIV)

Every age has unrighteousness as a core in its lifestyle, yet through grace we have access to His righteousness.

Righteousness exalts a nation, but sin condemns any people. (Proverbs 14:34 NIV)

If that's what it does to a nation it can do the same for the individual; the extent of its elevation and development of the Christian is endless. We should think and say those things that are pure and wholesome. We need not be accused of duplicity in our dealings, our yes should be yes and our no is no.

There was a time when to be a Christian assured any employer of a righteous employee. When l was a young Christian full of passion for Christ, during the boss's lunch break the men would read their papers, l would read the bible. One day the boss called me into his office and told me there had been a complaint about me doing this. He said, "As a Christian, you are stealing my time by not working during my absence" – this totally convicted me of my unrighteous behavior.

On leaving the office he said, "And l know of all the rest are reading their papers!" I never did it again or anything like it. After that, throughout my working life l walked the extra mile!

Context is everything. How could reading the bible be sinful? When the time is being paid to do something else. Reading the bible was not the sin – it was my thought process that it was OK to do this, that I was justified (maybe because of the behaviour of others) in dedicating this time to Christ. This experience taught me that our attitude – our thought behind our action – is what is vital in determining sin.

This is a critical distinction and one that, if modelled correctly, will provide the most support for the confusion that Christians often endure by misunderstanding sin as purely action. For example, imagine a person has picked up their suitcase from the airport but on the way out finds that they have mistakenly taken someone else's case. Are they in sin? The action would say they have stolen the case – but the thought was not for theft – there was no sinful thought or intent.

Now imagine a Christian that faithfully turns up at church each week, sings the hymns, gives the tithe, acts politely within the fellowship. But in their mind, they are filled with rage and jealousy – judgmental of everyone, absorbed in dark thoughts and intent toward others. Are they in sin? Oh, yes – most definitely. There are no actions or behaviours – but the thought is everything.

The fact is – sin is within!

Even in English law, there is a Latin tenet of inquiry – mens rea. It literally means 'with malice aforethought'. Even the laws of man distinguish the gravity of the 'thought' as well as the action - and punish such premeditation more punitively.

We need to not only preach but model righteousness in our conversations, lifestyle and relationships. We need to be of 'right-thought' – a clarity of mind that is open to our relationship with God and within which He may dwell.

Paul in Philippians 4:8 (NIV) says:

Finally, brothers and sisters, whatever is true, whatever is noble, whatever is right, whatever is pure, whatever is lovely, whatever is admirable – if anything is excellent or praiseworthy – think about such things.

Think about such things.

Imagine if we modelled these Christian values within our Church? Many people leave churches because they believe either the leadership and/or people are acting unrighteously (whether they are or not, it's the belief/thought that matters), or an offended person is not thinking righteously in the midst of their offence.

Just look at what Paul is sharing: basically, keep your thinking process fixed on these things.

Truth. Christ Himself is the foundation of all truth. The question is, do we always live it, tell it, believe it?

Nobility. Having or showing fine personal qualities or high moral principles. Uncorrupted, ethical, generous.

Right. Morally good, just, fair, virtuous, honest. Not being influenced by circumstances but acting impartially.

Pure. Not mixed or adulterated with other substances. Being in the world, but not of it! Not blending with the world.

Lovely. Having a beauty that appeals to the heart and mind.

Admirable. Arousing or deserving respect and approval. Credible, exemplary, worthy, deserving and worthwhile.

Excellent. Extremely good, outstanding, magnificent and first rate.

Praiseworthy. Commendable, laudable, deserving, exemplary.

In this list we see the outworking of a righteous person. But these outworkings come from an inner place – the engine-house of righteous thought.

Imagine if we spent time preaching the Jesus doctrine of righteousness. Imagine if each one of us studied these eight attributes of righteousness and grew in them all!

I ask the question, if we are commended to live righteous lives - are we doing it? What do we imagine righteousness to be?

I knew a Christian who was not yet divorced, but became pregnant from another man and declared, "The Lord knew I wanted a child!" No! Sin had entered the camp and deception had taken over. Was it the action of bearing a child that was sinful? Of course not. It was the thought that was formed long before the child. The intention to enter into a sinful union far preceded the outcome. The child is without sin. The parent is attempting to assuage sin by negotiating a distorted view of grace.

What about gossip? The cancer of the soul, inoperable, it needs confessing not deliverance. Gossip is not about words. Words are not sinful. It is the intention behind those words. Gossip seeks to sensationalise and titillate. It is designed for drama and theatre – to provide the bearer with the power of entertainment and intrigue. And those who participate – those who listen intently – become the bearers of the thought, the carriers of the virus. The gossip spreads – adding a little here and there to embellish the tale – the sin seeping out of every syllable. Destruction of thought made flesh in the audible. I have known many good people destroyed by the cancer of gossip – lies and a little knowledge thrown in to engender plausibility – families shamed and scorned for no other purpose than the spreading of sin.

James, who speaks on wisdom, also comments on righteousness

"Peacemakers who sow in peace, reap a harvest of righteousness." (James 3:18 NIV)

The truth is, not many people receive teaching on this subject. When we saw considerable growth in the early life of Renewal, people turned to Christ weekly and dramatically; families and teenagers by the dozen. We needed to teach these people the tenets of their new faith, so we had a sixteen-week programme that contained virtually every teaching that Jesus had either personally delivered, intimated, or that the apostles had revealed. It was called 'Foundation of Faith". One church member came in and completed the course three consecutive times before becoming its teacher. He is now an Elder of the Church and was the Director of our Bible Training Institute.

That was a long time ago – in the days of pen and paper and speaking person to person, in a classroom. In this age of communication, it should be so much easier to podcast or DVD all the training needed to disciple a transient people who live and work often miles away from their 'local Church'.

Where we had to write on paper, photocopy and personally deliver each lecture for sixteen weeks, now, they could select any subject and watch it anywhere in the world! Yet often, today, we can't find the same commitment.

I think you are getting the message; righteousness is the fundamental outcome of those who have been forgiven of sin and who await future judgment. It is the antidote to death and hell. It's vital that we pursue it, hold on to it and confess it.

He that followeth after righteousness and mercy findeth life, righteousness and honour.

(Proverbs 21:21 KJV)

May we all do just that!

3

JUDGMENT

This is from where we derive crisis; to make a decision, subjectively or objectively, for or against. A tribunal by implication (especially Divine law) - accusation, condemnation, damnation.

It would be true to say that many of the 21st Century Churches would not consider it comfortable to deliver a sermon that even implied the risk of its hearers facing accusations, condemnation and, if you are like some well-known Evangelical leaders, damnation!

Paul however, speaking of life in Christ, openly confesses that there is now no condemnation for those who are in Christ Jesus. We must stop here a little while. For those who are in Christ Jesus, he didn't say there was no longer condemnation, rather that it was no longer an appropriate reference to those who had been convicted by the Holy Spirit of sin and responded to His righteousness - because by so doing they had immunised themselves from the consequences of the judgment to come.

The importance here is that those who refuse His righteousness are still under the consequences of the judgment of God. They key phrase in this is 'in Christ Jesus'. The prayer of Christ in John 17 is the unity of Christ in the Father and the Christian in Christ "that they may be one as we are one"

So, if we are to believe that the Holy Spirit is commissioned to convict people of their standing before Almighty God and their acceptance or rejection of His Son Jesus Christ, then we must believe that the preaching of this is the personification of true seeker friendliness.

Jesus told us, When He comes, He (The Holy Spirit) will lead us into all truth (John 16:13)

In this statement He is telling us, as He is Truth, the Holy Spirit leads us to Christ, who reconciles us to the Father.

So, Christianity is not a good idea but a God idea; it is a responsive faith, the Holy Spirit convicting us of Sin. It's then up to us to decide what we wish to do with that revelation.

The evangelical approach to a 'sinner's prayer' may result in people being converted, even when it's not a biblical concept. There are many ways that people start their journey that are not necessarily biblical concepts (for instance, nowhere in the bible is it suggested that a church parent and toddler group would be a conduit to conversion – however I know many for whom this was the start of their journey) but to convey to people that a simple prayer engages the total and complete gospel is to cheapen the whole concept of the Jesus doctrine. It's a start. That's all. The journey continues.

John Bunyan's work Pilgrims Progress is a classic work of allegory, much like the latter day 'Lord of the Rings'. Charles Spurgeon, the famous Baptist preacher said of it, "Next to the bible, the book I value is Pilgrims Progress"

Augustus Toplady - the hymn writer said, "It's a masterpiece of piety and genius; and will, we doubt not, be of standing use to the people of God so long as the sun and moon endure"

You can get it in modern English if you are hampered by the language of old England. But for those unfamiliar, the Pilgrim is on a journey to find the Celestial City. The struggles and experiences that he encounters along the journey could have so easily deterred him from completion. This graphic story shows in pictorial language the journey that most of us face if we subscribe to the Jesus doctrine.

Jesus commanded us to, "Go and make disciples" and this instruction gives us the concept of shaping, fashioning, creating. Disciples are disciplined learners, this doesn't happen in the emotion of a single meeting or one encounter alone. That can be the start of the journey – and a significant start it can be – but it's not enough on its own.

The salvation process according to the doctrines of Jesus must redeem the fourfold manifestation of the human creation.

You must love The Lord your God with all your mind, body, soul and spirit - yourself, your neighbor, those who despitefully abuse you and your enemies.

Love and forgiveness are the traits of a redeemed life. When asked what the traits of a believer are, Jesus replied, "by their fruit you shall know them"

So, it's love, joy, peace, forbearance, kindness, goodness, faithfulness, gentleness, self-control (Galatians 5 v22-23). These are the core characteristics of a Christian.

So, Christianity is a fruit-bearing longevity. It is not secured for eternity by a thirty second prayer.

The Apostle Paul identifies with this, telling his readers that he had kept the faith, run the race and fought the good fight, so, there was laid up for him his reward. Jesus makes it so clear that Christianity is a lifetime commitment with eternal consequences,

He who puts his hand to the plough and looks back, is not fit for the Kingdom of God. (Luke 9:62)

You may well be thinking the same as the disciples when they said, "Who then can be saved?" (Luke 18:26). This came when Jesus made the statement to a rich young ruler after he enquired "Good teacher, what shall I do to inherit eternal life?"

This was a moral young man who had endeavoured to live by the commandments yet had no assurance of eternal life. He was not condemned by The Lord for his morality; Jesus actually loved him and was impressed by his character.

This young man was one of the few that understood the need for eternal life. He actually sought his inheritance - a gift of what Christ would give upon His death. What a revelation! Jesus who was eternal life, dying to give an inheritance.

The answer was not to pray a prayer but, "Sell all that you have and distribute to the poor, and you will have treasures in heaven, and come, follow Me" (Matthew 19:21)

Jesus said to the disappointed young man "How hard it is for those who have riches to enter the kingdom of God?" He then gives the illustration of a camel passing through the eye of a needle.

This can mean either one of two things: -

Literally the impossibility of one who puts riches or anything else before Christ entering the Kingdom.

A camel that was loaded with goods could not enter through the gate of the City unless it was first unloaded. We cannot enter the gateway of eternity when retaining the baggage of time. If we want to engage into His nature we must first die to our old nature, we must enter free from our baggage!

This is not assaulting riches. Money is not evil, it's the love of money that is the root; foundational footings of evil. Mammon is a spiritual manifestation in economic form. Zacchaeus broke that control by firstly obeying the Jewish law of restitution (we will return to this later) and then giving by a voluntary basis half of his wealth to feed the poor, which is grace.

So, Jesus Christ fulfilled both law and grace. That in itself is salvation. That is why Jesus said to him, "Salvation has come to this house". Jesus fulfilled the law of God by dying for fallen man and then saved us by Grace.

I hear some say, "Can I lose my salvation?" I personally would say no – but you can choose to give it away. If there is true repentance, the Lord is waiting to receive His own. The story of the prodigal son demonstrates this well.

The story starts with two sons, one (approaching thirty) asks for his inheritance which is his by right. He leaves his father's house and spends it on self-centered and self-gratifying things. After a time of living an independent lifestyle he degenerates into a depraved individual who would have gladly eaten the food of swine. For a Jew, this is as low as it gets!

We now see the defining moment of the story; he comes to a realisation that his life outside of Father is void and pointless. He assesses that even the lowest servant has a better lifestyle than himself. He decides to return to the father in a repentant and unworthy state, no longer worthy of 'son ship'. The father in the meantime is looking for him (remember the Lord, looking for Adam in Eden). This shows the love and devotion that God has for those whom He personally loves.

Seeing his son returning, he runs to meet him, embracing him and, hearing his confession, he makes this statement: "My son was dead and is alive again, lost but now found", notice this statement 'dead and lost' before repentance changed and engaged the mercy of God.

The son was washed, clothed in righteousness, had a ring of son ship, sandals of peace and a feast of reconciliation. However, he never had returned to him the inheritance he lost. This was seen in the father's conversation with the complaining brother who thought he would be receiving back the inheritance he had squandered.

There are, therefore, key messages in this story, according to the father his son was both lost and dead until the son "came to his senses". But the son was not 'rewarded' for his unrighteousness – he was not given a second inheritance to squander – but he was welcomed back into the arms of the Father.

We are on a journey. Christianity is a lifetime of lifestyle. It needs the injection of daily meditation and personal integrity. Jesus was making it very clear that true salvation comes by His Grace, yet Grace does not excuse wilful sin and premeditated unrighteousness. Remember – it's the thought that counts!

The Condition of the Church

And because lawlessness will be increased, the love of many will grow cold. But the one who endures to the end will be saved. (Matthew 24:12-13 ESV)

Lawlessness has a meaning of not knowing or acknowledging the law. This can be seen in today's generation. Both secular and spiritual boundaries - or moral ethics that the church promotes - are to be vigorously opposed.

The strength of the Christian Church is found in its vitality during opposition; we need however to take stock, to see if the viability is within our spiritual structure, or will it be subject to damage.

In well-known scripture, Jesus speaks of how the love of many people will grow cold. The inference of "grow" is that it is over a period of time. The call is to endure to the end, so bringing salvation. This is not a gospel of works or luck, this is a gospel of His Kingdom. It's full of faithfulness, endurance and obedience; the essential qualities needed to maintain the Church as His future Bride.

The Church is His, obviously, yet sometimes this may be forgotten in the rush of serving. We, by His grace, develop a consistency and a desire to maintain the race of life, a commitment to maintain the faith and to fight a good fight against the ploys of the enemy. It is our response to His eternal offer of Salvation that determines our final destiny. When we see the sacrificial lifestyle of many believers, often facing persecution, rejection and even death, one is compelled to ask the question, why is there a considerable difference between armchair Christianity and that of Crucified Christianity?

Hebrews 11 speaks of transforming faith that produces both progressive testimony of receiving grace and those who the scripture states, "chose a better resurrection", whatever this truly means.

These people wandered distressed in the wilderness naked, even being cut in two. The thought is horrid! Yet today in the world, the church is again seeing martyrdom in increasing ways.

The scripture then says, "that this world was not worthy of them".

A costless gospel is inevitably a crossless gospel. Christianity therefore is truly a work of God's Grace; we receive it by faith during repentance and then it is maintained by the indwelling of the Spirit.

For those Christians who say, 'we don't need to belong to a Church to be Christian' they are deluding themselves and showing deep ignorance of the Word. If your experience precludes your active participation in the Church, you are living outside of covenant relationship. True discipleship is community, it's interdependency of faith blending in relationship with others.

The Ecclesia 'called out' is full of people at various stages of growth; brothers and sisters, prophets and other apostolic giftings and elders. Yes, we all battle with the old nature. Paul reminds the believers gathered that we must die daily, yet each day we must dwell in the resurrected power of His Spirit

Paul is figuratively beating his body into submission. No, not flailing like the monks of old, but personal spiritual discipline, bringing thoughts and, subsequently, actions of the flesh into control of the Holy Spirit. It's true that Churches are full of people who struggle, yet cooperatively we can live in ease of obedience.

The Church through the writings of John in Revelation faces many challenges. The Lord tells of those in the last days who are rejected, even though they attempt to justify themselves through prophecies and teachings. He will say to those who are not born of the Spirit, "Depart from Me you workers of iniquity, 1 never knew you". In this case, iniquity is willful sin. It's having charisma without character, gifting without Godliness, signs without servanthood, works without the word, self-certification without self-crucifixion.

We are the bride of the coming Christ. So many of the parables major on the end of times that we, the Church, need to be circumspect in our actions and our teachings.

We mustn't be like the foolish virgins. In this parable they are all virgins, sadly all slept, yet the acid test was who had oil? You can have incredible values as a religious person, yet do you have the fullness of the Holy Spirit? When the shout came, "the Groom is coming" it was the defining time of reflection. Those without His light tried to buy oil, today we would try denominations, local church, charities and philanthropic organisations. Yet the outcome was, "Go away, 1 don't know you"

This is serious. In all Churches, including my own, there are adherents who are in agreement with the purpose of the Church, yet, have no oil! We have a duty to warn them before the Call!

Are we at differing stages of Christian growth? Yes, we are all part of a family differing in maturity.

When Jesus said to man, "you must be born again" it was the start of a life. It starts with a spiritual conception, then birth, pediatric care leading to puberty, then maturity.

The Apostle Paul described it this way, "when 1 was a child 1 thought like a child, acted as a child...yet 1 have now put away childish things" (1 Corinthians 13:11). He continued that often he would have wished to give them the meat of the word, however, they still needed milk! Are you getting the message?

Churches must not lose the message of biblical Christianity. Last year l was preaching in Nigeria. A young PhD Pastor asked to see me after a lecture. He shared his deep concern that as some of the Senior Pastors who preached a theological depth had retired, they had been increasingly replaced by motivational preaching that lacked the theological discipline for the long team health of the Church, there is obviously no harm in positive thinking, but we should not be deceived into believing that this is a substitute for Christian thinking.

For as he thinketh in his heart, so is he: Eat and drink, saith he to thee; but his heart is not with thee. (Proverbs 23:7 KJV)

Norman Vincent Peel, in his book "The Power of Positive Thinking" has taken the bible and published a book based on its principles. It has sold more than seven million copies in fifteen languages. To those who read it, it can change their thought pattern and many have adopted these Christian principles, yet have never met nor committed themselves to Christ.

Therefore, Churches can so easily fall into the same trap; base our sermons on scriptures yet see little or no conviction of the Holy Spirit. Positive thinking mixed with faith teaching can, if not monitored, bring people into a denial of reality. Anything that seems negative is often banned as unproductive. However, what some call negative, others would rightly call challenging.

Yes, we should be comprehensive in our subject material, yet not at the exclusion of traditional theological teaching.

The church l have Pastored for forty-five years was, at its height, noted as being founded on the Word; a twenty-week series on the "Tabernacle and the Temple" the revelation of the nature and ministry of Christ, then thirty weeks on the Creed, the basic tenets of our faith, twelve weeks on the Lord's Prayer coupled with a CD of thirteen songs composed and sung by my close friend Dave Cooper; then a series on the fruit of the Spirit followed by ten weeks on the Commandments. This was not an easy time to sit in church. These were long and challenging series with depth of teaching. Attending church could even have been considered hard work as together we grappled with the wider issues of biblical teaching. But with it (and, I believe because of it) we grew to be the largest Church in our region; recognising the importance of the Word, the Freedom of the Holy Spirit and the relevance of our Worship.

You could call it thematic preaching however the subjects contained the fundamentals of our faith. These sermons came directly from the bible. There was no need for motivational style business techniques or 'feel good' themes. You may feel that I'm a little paranoid about the style of preaching.

It's not that at all. In the past, l was a successful businessman managing hundreds of professional footballers. It was through this, as a motivational speaker travelling to cities in many parts of the world, that brought its own earthly rewards. I mixed with many leading speakers staying at hotels such as Boca Rotan Florida, Hotel de Paris Monte Carlo, Princess Hamilton Bermuda, Fairmont Le Montreux Palace Switzerland, even travelling on the Orient Express. And through this experience I can immediately recognise the difference between Christ-centric preaching and Christian motivational speaking. A Christ-centric philosophy is the only basis of the Apostle Paul's incredible insight into the heart and mind of the Almighty.

Of course, we can give practical everyday advice on lifestyle, yet superficiality of doctrine or restricted doctrine leaves the hearer at least unbalanced, at worst spiritually deficient. It's not enough to know what to do – it's more about knowing how to be; how to be in right-thought, of right-mind, of right-spirit of right-heart.

We should first take biblical truth and then decide its delivery. We can't do it the other way around. Dreaming up a theatrical format that we then try to squash within some theology is never going to work. We simply bend and distort the truth to fit the scenery. And we must never, ever, decide what is acceptable based on public opinion. This is as much seen among the traditional wing of the church as it is with the Charismatics.

As explained in the section on the Communion/Eucharist this can either become the central theological expression of Orthodox Church - or the Word or Worship in the Evangelical, Charismatic Church. We of course need all three of these with the addition of prayer.

Our treatment of visitors is vitally important, hospitality is a cornerstone of Christian life and how we care for others represents our heart for the lost and our fellowship. However, if the hospitality contrives the experiential – if the temperature or quality of the coffee, the lighting and platform presentation, the costumes and the props rival the spiritual expectations, then we have lost the reason for the season!

People will respond to the depth of our message. Biblical truth is not about blame or judgment (judge not, says the bible) and this is where wisdom is needed. The depth of truth will challenge a seeker from within, not from without. Aggression is not needed (which then calls for a defensive stance from the hearer) – just truth, without distortion or sanctimony.

However, sinners are not seekers until they have been exposed to the fullness of the gospel and the conviction of the Holy Spirit. There is a myth that you can't teach serious doctrine with humour and relevant illustrations. But Jesus did it in the parables of His day. He was a storyteller – He spoke so that the people would understand, in a way that held their attention and convicted their hearts and minds. This is a skill that preachers would do well to emulate – to learn from the way in which Jesus connected with the people – without a building, a coffee pot or a projector to be seen.

Those who enter the Kingdom at differing levels manifest different levels of maturity. Those who are exposed to the 'Jesus doctrine' mature quicker than those who have been exposed to a lesser spiritual experience. And when I talk of maturity, I am in no way relating this to time. A Christian can have been 'saved' for decades and still be immature in their faith – whereas their neighbour could be saved a year and demonstrating great maturity for their time within Christ. Maturity is a matter of attitude and understanding – the speed and power of 'right-thought' in manifesting within their life.

I am not in any way advocating any form of legalistic living, just the opposite. Be it a traditional or contemporary approach to church, the bible needs to be the central focus of all our lifestyles.

So Church is made up of those who have been convicted of sin. It is then, on this conviction, that the individual enters into a lifetime of commitment.

The Christians gained their name at Antioch, as they manifested the lifestyle and the anointing of Christ the Anointed One. It is therefore a sad reflection when Mahatma Gandhi said, "I like your Christ, I do not like your Christians. Your Christians are so unlike your Christ"

We, as Christians, must be images of our Christ.

St Augustine of Hippo said, "Because God has made us for Himself, our hearts are restless until they rest in Him"

It is this journey of St Paul, he who needed a daily dying, yet also a daily resurrection, that enabled him to engage the power of the Holy Spirit. By conforming in His death enabled Paul to die to sin because Christ had died for sin. Paul recognised that His sacrifice was once for all, no temple ritual but rather a daily experience of transformation.

The Church message needs to qualify that true Christianity is not a take it or leave it faith. It takes nothing less than complete surrender to Christ. It isn't destined to be totally acceptable to all

– it cannot be styled for contemporary culture – modified through the ages to suit the zeitgeist.

True Christianity is only accessed by a narrow Gate...few actually find it.

G K Chesterton, in "What's Wrong with the World", said,

"The Christian ideal has not been tried and found wanting. It has been found difficult; and left untried."

With Jesus declaring that the faith of many will fail in the latter days, many more will give heed to false doctrines and be turned to error. False Christs or anointings will arise. This doesn't mean they will claim to be the Messiah, but they manifest anointing. Lifting-up ministry rather than Christ, it will be drawing attention to self. True Christian ministry doesn't produce platform stars, it produces humility.

Charles H Spurgeon said, "You will never glory in God till first of all God has killed your glorifying in yourself."

Richard Roar said, in "Breathing Underwater; Spirituality and the 12 steps"

"Christians are usually sincere and well-intentioned people until you get to any real issues of ego, control, power, money, pleasure and security. Then they tend to be pretty much like anybody else".

As Christians we should not be described in such a way, however, without living in the "Jesus doctrine" we do seem to be no different to the world. We must guard against a bogus version of the gospel, a fast food alternative that satisfies the soullessness of man without transforming who he is. When the Cross overshadowed by culture, the gospel becomes tainted by consumerism and legalism.

That might be hard hitting and not typically true of all, however there is a growing 'fast food' mentality that has affected the eating habits of some churches. When returning to the book of Hebrews, chapter eleven, we see that many preachers have well-worn the first half of this popular chapter, yet few preachers have exalted the latter part, where in verse 35 we read, "Others were tortured, not accepting deliverance, that they might obtain a better resurrection"

It then lists those who suffered mocking, scourging, were put in chains, slain with the sword, imprisoned, stoned, sawn in two, tempted, left destitute, afflicted and tormented. Those who wandered about in sheepskins and goat skins in the desert and mountains, dens and caves, of whom the world was not worthy.

These are an important part of the Church, and many more in this are experiencing such trials, yet often in western churches, little is said to prepare people for the future.

Throughout the last two thousand years, the Christian faith has been afflicted with persecution and opposition.

In 2015, I visited Rome. At the burial place of Paul, the priest said to us, "Look at the hill next to Paul's grave, what do you think it is?" We didn't know, so he explained that after Caesar had sanctioned Paul's beheading, he turned to his army and confronted his soldiers. He challenged them that if they had a Christian faith, unless they denied it, they would be beheaded. That hill was the burial ground for the ten thousand who removed their armour and waited to be martyred for their emerging faith.

I was deeply moved. I had never known this story. A modern designer faith would not have sustained those martyrs; the depth of their love for Christ made that mass slaughter a Hebrews 11 reality.

As previously stated, it's not my intention to promote a faith of 'flailing and suffering'. It is, however, my intention to reveal a faith that for centuries has birthed Martyrs and genuine Saints who did not see Christianity as Social inclusion but often exclusion. All these historic Christians, and especially those in the Wesley

Revival, saw their faith as a lifetime experience and not just a quick prayer and filling in a follow-up form!

It was enduring to the end with no turning back; denial and leaving are not biblical qualities of redeemed people.

The paradox with many 'brands' of Christianity is the extremity of the personal standing of the individual Christian. On the one side we have those expressing that, as part of Abraham's seed, they are entitled to all his promises, prosperity and governance. On the other side we are at best unworthy; sinners begging for crumbs of redemption

Wealth or Woe is me!

We seek classification of a biased doctrine of either extreme prosperity or poverty mentality. The Church needs to teach balance.

In Philippians 4:12 NASB1995 Paul says thus,

"I know how to get along with humble means, and 1 also know how to live in prosperity; in any and every circumstance 1 have learned the secret of being filled and going hungry, both of having abundance and suffering need..."

Paul facing persecution only has this concern, "if only 1 may finish my course with joy and ministry which 1 have obtained" (Acts 20:24)

If we are to survive as Christians in this society of humanistic and pluralistic influence, we need mature and balanced teaching.

"It is Jesus that you seek when you dream of happiness; He is waiting for you when nothing else you find satisfies you; He is the beauty to which you are so attracted; it is He who reads in your heart your most genuine choices, the choice that others try to stifle. It is Jesus who sits in you the desire to do something great with your lives, the will to follow an ideal, the refusal to allow yourselves to be ground down by mediocrity, the courage to commit yourselves humbly

and patiently to improving yourselves and society; making the world more human and more fraternal"
(Pope John Paul II)

Did you get that?

"It's Jesus you seek when you dream of happiness" not a new BMW or a worldwide Ministry.

The early Church had a true Community attitude to faith; all things in common and meeting the need of those in want, continuing in the Apostles doctrine and in the breaking of bread. To these people, there were additional converts added daily. Cultural gospels are obvious, it's man interpreting faith through the lens of tradition or even perceived lack of it. Every culture is influenced by tradition, fashion or fad, be it choral music with its robes and set liturgy or the Charismatic with its jeans and open necked shirt - and worship set timed to perfection.

The Churches of true imagination can call on the various expressions of tradition and weave them into Worship and lifestyle... remember, today's 'free spirit' is tomorrow's tradition!

So, the Church of the twenty-first Century needs wisdom; yes displaying cultural packaging, yet retaining the values, theology and doctrines not of the early church, but of the church. The Nicene Creed formulated in AD 325 has no need of rewriting. The Apostles' Creed, AD 390, is also the bedrock of Christian belief.

Jesus said, "I will build My Church and the gates of hell will not prevail against it".
(Matthew 16: 18)

Let us therefore join Him in the task of seeing that Church multiply within our areas of influence

REDEMPTION & RANSOM

I'm going to start with some Greek words:

agoras - to purchase in the marketplace

exagorazo - going from something to something, as Christians from bondage to freedom

lutroo - to obtain release by the payment of a price

Knowing that you were ransomed from the futile ways inherited from your forefathers, not with perishable things such as silver or gold, but with the precious blood of Christ, like that of a lamb without blemish or spot. (1 Peter 1:18-19 ESV)

Jesus was both uncompromising in his message yet compassionate in his relationships. He called sin as it was and never lowered the bar of acceptance to the level of human acceptability. He died a horrific death to save humanity from a horrendous conclusion to life.

Death outside of Christ was indescribable. You can understand why it is easy to believe in Universalism. We rationalise the bible and develop a systematic philosophy of a 'feel-good' syndrome. It becomes the manual for positive thinking and good resolutions, without the thoughts that may offend, challenge, convict and condemn.

We are not saved from negativity we are saved from sin. Paul argues that in Christ sin shall not have dominion over us, which of course indicates that outside of Christ it will.

Paul speaks about us being redeemed or ransomed or atonement; to recover ownership by paying a specific sum, to set free, rescue, ransom, to restore the honour, worth or reputation, to release a person in return for a payment of a demanded price...to deliver from sin and its consequences.

But when the fullness of time had come, God sent forth his Son, born of woman, born under the law, to redeem those who were under the law, so that we might receive adoption as sons. And because you are sons, God has sent the Spirit of his Son into our hearts, crying, "Abba! Father!"
(Galatians 4:4-6 ESV)

Paul is explaining that Jesus was born of a woman so placing himself under the same potential to sin; he was God born into human flesh, subject to temptation as we see in the wilderness. Yet He overcame the temptation to sin. The law said that all who sin shall die (Ezekiel 18:20) and to qualify it, "all have sinned and fallen short of his glory" (Romans 3:23)

He, the Christ, redeemed humanity, paid the cost of the innocent for the guilty and in so redeeming, buying back the relationship lost by corruption and turning it into true son ship with the Father.

Christ redeemed us from the curse of the law by becoming a curse for us—for it is written, "Cursed is everyone who is hanged on a tree"— so that in Christ Jesus the blessing of Abraham might come to the Gentiles, so that we might receive the promised Spirit through faith. (Galatians 3:13-14 ESV)

Paul calls the law a curse. Basically, the law had limitations. It could only reveal truth and sin, it could not redeem us from the penalty of sin, it was merely a check list of righteousness.

By Jesus Christ dying on the cross, he appropriated the curse of His day. No Roman citizen was crucified, that is why Paul was beheaded.

The cure of sin was turned into the blessings of Abraham to all gentiles. So, the redemption message was one of restoration: not to what we used to be (we were born in sin) but to what we were intended to be.

That is a great thought, think about it: redeemed and ransomed so that you may become what is impossible for you to become outside of Him who paid the price we did not qualify to pay.

Knowing that you were ransomed from the futile ways inherited from your forefathers, not with perishable things such as silver or gold, (1 Peter 1:18 ESV)

Peter joins in the discussion, there is no earthly currency that can 'purchase' our pardon...silver, gold or aimless conduct received by the tradition of your fathers....that can be either human philosophy or even religious practice. Someone needed to meet the outstanding demands for freedom, Jesus was the 'Lamb who takes away the sin of the World'.

The fact that the values of this world, the silver and gold, could not redeem us shows that our redemption was not contrived on earth but in heaven. Sin demands death as its penalty. Since the garden of Eden, this has been seen as the antidote for sin, the death of the innocent for the guilty.

The Old Covenant saw lambs by the multitude becoming a sin offering. Yet one day by a river, John the baptiser saw Jesus Christ walking towards him. Seeing Him, John cries with a loud voice

'The Lamb of God who takes away the sin of the World'. One final lamb without spot or blemish.

Jesus, knowing the severity of such an action, asks the Father for alternative opportunities. "If it be Thy will let this cup pass from me" yet He qualifies it by saying "Yet not My will but Yours be done". Redemption is beyond a simple prayer of sorrow. It's even beyond the tears of a contrite heart. Before we actually responded to the conviction of the Holy Spirit, He paid the price for my covenanted freedom. It is Godly sorrow that leads to repentance.

And they sang a new song, saying,

"Worthy are you to take the scroll and to open its seals, for you were slain, and by your blood you ransomed people for God from every tribe and language and people and nation"

(Revelation 5:9 ESV)

We often hear that, one day, those who are truly Christian, both those who have passed into eternal time and those who are earth bound will sing a new song as unto The Lord. 'And You have redeemed us to God by Your blood out of every tribe and tongue and people and nation, and have made us Kings and priests to our God'

So, in this combined new song we will celebrate our redemption. We must not trivialise the need for redemption. At the age of 42 I had a heart attack. I didn't take it seriously until my consultant, Dr Murray, said to me, "Mr Carr, if you don't change your lifestyle, you will be dead in six months!" That was 30 years ago.

There comes a time when you must talk seriously and not see it as negative or offensive but lifesaving. Dr. Murray didn't like telling me that, however it saved my life. He didn't speak with condemnation in his voice but with concern for my future wellbeing. Again, we can learn from the truth of doctors!

Job, in the midst of personal disaster, not only recognises his chronic disastrous position, but in his quotation confirms the need for a redeemer:

"For I know that my redeemer lives" (Job 19:25 NKJV)

"The redeemer will come to Zion, and to those who turn from transgressions in Jacob"
(Job 19:25 NKJV)

Easton's bible dictionary describes redemption as a work of salvation, as a rescue from the bondage of sin; rescue by a payment accomplished by the payment or price, deliverance considered as a ransom or repurchase.

Satisfaction vicaria - vicarious satisfaction – in that Christ was considered legitimate payment for the atoning of sin.

Paul correctly considers that as we have been "bought with a price" we are to honour Him with our bodies...or glorify. Basically, reflect who He is and manifest His beauty in the midst of apathy and indifference. (1 Corinthians 6:20)

We have been "bought with a price" - do not become slaves to human beings.

We are not to become captured by human relationships that may bring bondage to the things of the living God. (1 Corinthians 7:23)

Now there is a final reason I think that Jesus says "Love your enemies"

It is this; that love has within it a redemptive power. And there is a power there that eventually transforms individuals...Just keep being friendly to that person. Just keep loving them, and they can't stand it too long.

Oh, they react in many ways in the beginning. They react with guilt feelings, and sometimes they'll hate a little more at that transition period, but just keep loving them...And by the power of your love they will break down under the load.

That love, you see, - It is redemptive, and this is why Jesus is love. There's something about love that builds up and is creative. There is something about hate that tears down and is destructive. So love your enemies.

"A Knock at Midnight; Inspirations from the Great Sermons of Reverend Martin Luther King Jr."

Isn't that what actually happened to each and every one of us in our relationship with Christ Jesus? It was by His love that we experienced redemptive power, and some yes, actually hated Him, yet He so loved the World that He gave His only begotten Son that whosoever believes in Him should not perish [die] but have everlasting life. (John 3:16).

He paid the price by death yet sown in love and administered by compassion through Grace. He loved us, favoured us, saved us, adopted us, redeemed us.

We never value our salvation if we do not appreciate the act of Redemption and Ransom. He both redeemed us, bought us back, and paid the ransom with the shedding of His own blood.

He substituted Himself in the firing line instead of us - the innocent for the guilty.

"If a man had his way, the plan of redemption would be an endless and bloody conflict. In reality, salvation was bought not by Jesus' first, but by His nail-pieced hands; not by muscle but by love; not by vengeance but by forgiveness; not by force but by sacrifice. Jesus Christ our Lord surrendered in Order that He might win; he destroyed His enemies by dying for them and conquered death by allowing death to conquer Him" ("Preparing for Jesus' Return: Daily Live the Blessed Hope" – A W Tozer)

The act of Redemption may have become physically evidenced at the Cross-, yet we know the eternity of God pre constructed our restoration before even the world began....

The will of God was that no one should perish [die and be spiritually void of eternal bliss] yet making man with leadership and ruler ship gives humanity the choice of redemption or rejection...

"God allows man to learn His supernatural ends, but the decision to strive towards an end, the choice of course, is left to man's free will. God does not redeem man against his will"

(Pope Paul II)

Love and Responsibility

We live in a time not different to ages past that hostage taking has maintained its high profile.

It imprisons a person, restricting freedom and liberty. It isolates and deprives one of a normal and free lifestyle. It demands a payment of great significance. Sin and death have taken hostage the human soul and threaten to kill, maim and imprison it. There was no other who could pay the price of sin; Christ asked for the cup of suffering to pass from Him, however knowing, as in the words of the Hymn:

"There was no other good enough to pay the price of sin, He only could unlock the gates of Heaven and let us in"

He paid the ransom; with His life and body bearing the abuse of our captivity. The marks of death and hell manifesting themselves publicly and unashamedly upon Him, yet even in carrying the consequences of our failure upon His body He turned His whipped bleeding back into the confirmation of our healing because, "by His stripes we are healed". Unless we grasp this concept of Him buying our freedom by His own life, then we will never appreciate the depth of His love for us as individuals.

In 1 Corinthians 6:20 Paul says as you have been redeemed with a price; glorify God in your body and spirit. Simply live a life both spiritually and practically that brings credit and worship to him and not to us.

In chapter 7:23 Paul continues to explain that our redemption frees us from the captivity to man, we are no longer to be dominated or enslaved by others.

Be it emotional or psychological or even physical, we are not to live in the fear of man, but rather the freedom of Christ.

I don't see much of this teaching within the discipleship of new Christians today; there seems little if any appreciation of the need and then the cost of salvation and the means of achieving it. There seems to be a philosophy of gradually growing into a lifestyle rather than being born into it and then growing into it.

Redemption is however a purchasing of one's soul by the sacrifice of Christ, "You were bought with a price" and we therefore are not our own; true Christianity is retaining one's ability to make decisions, without independence from the will of the Holy Spirit.

Freedom through a ransom always demands a cost, the higher the profile of the person the more costly the ransom, therefore the fact that it demanded the death of God's only begotten Son for all of humanity reveals the value The Lord placed on every one of us.

In Judaism, ransom is called kofer-nefesh. The word was applied to the poll tax of a half shekel to be paid by every male above twenty years at the census. A dictionary definition is ideal for the likeness of the human soul in relationship to sin. To redeem a prisoner, slave, kidnapped person, of captured goods. It's a means of deliverance or rescue from punishment, incorporating the many analogies given in the scriptures we who have been imprisoned by sin can be set free.

The Hymn writer Charles Wesley puts it graphically in an extract from the hymn "And Can it be that I should Gain":

"...long my imprisoned spirit lay fast bound in sin and nature's night:

Thine eye diffused a quickening ray-
I woke, the dungeon flamed with light;
My chains fell off, my heart was free,
I rose, went forth, and followed Thee.

Redemption is not only being redeemed from something it is being redeemed to something.

Who redeems your life from destruction: who crowns you with loving-kindness and tender mercies. (Psalm 103:4 NKJV)

So, after the act of atonement comes the adorning of the crown of abundant love mingled with kindness, impregnated with tender mercy.

The poverty of sin is replaced by the prosperity of His Grace. There is a gratefulness that grows within the heart and life of those who have experienced redemption and been truly ransomed from the captivity of sin. So, we would do well to explain to new converts the depth of the salvation they have entered into.

JUSTIFICATION & SANCTIFICATION

Behold the proud,
His soul is not upright in him;
But the just shall live by his faith.
(Habakkuk 2:4 NKJV)

The just shall live...those who have become lawful, no longer under the condemnation of the law within which they had been judged unworthy. The transaction that had transferred them from being unrighteous to righteous, the prayers of a righteous fervent man that avails much.

It's living in a lifestyle of freedom, no longer under the condemnation of sin, but manifesting a freedom that transforms the individual from a negative relationship with the Almighty into one of boldness mingled with humility.

Paul said, in his letter to the Romans 1:16-17 ESV:

For I am not ashamed of the gospel, for it is the power of God for salvation to everyone who believes, to the Jew first and also to the

Greek. For in it the righteousness of God is revealed from faith for faith, as it is written, "The righteous shall live by faith."

Paul is no longer either embarrassed or offended with the Gospel of Christ; it is a power to salvation for everyone who believes, yes to every believer there is a power surge. This gospel justifies the sinner, brings them into the righteousness of God And implants the faith of God into the believer to have faith in God their Saviour. In simpler terms, He justifies His actions towards us, by changing us to the extent that we now receive the abundance of His grace and mercy without feeling totally unworthy. We can stand boldly in His presence based on the total work He has performed in our lives. He became my unworthiness so that I might receive His worthiness.

and are justified by his grace as a gift, through the redemption that is in Christ Jesus, whom God put forward as a propitiation by his blood, to be received by faith. This was to show God's righteousness, because in his divine forbearance he had passed over former sins. It was to show his righteousness at the present time, so that he might be just and the justifier of the one who has faith in Jesus. (Romans 3:24-26 ESV)

These scriptures are loaded with incredible truths that, if not explained to new Christians will condemn them to superficiality. It has never been easy to describe the incredible process of our salvation, however, to gloss it over with a simple worship song or "experience" is so dangerous to the longevity of the Christian.

I, who through Dyslexia could not read or write properly until my late teens, was still taught the reality of such a deep and lasting experience of Christ's Salvation. I've talked of my brother, Michael, and his teaching – giving a depth of insight into the richness of the scriptures. When I sat listening to him I didn't fully understand the significance of it, or to be truthful the logic of it, however when I was filled with the Holy Spirit all his teachings fell trifold into place - firstly they flooded back to me, secondly I understood them, and thirdly they transformed my theology.

Paul is saying in this scripture that we have been 'justified' - made acceptable to the Father by His grace (unmerited favour) through redemption (being bought back by the sacrifice of His Son) who God had already planned the perfect solution for our rescue...by the blood of Christ. And all this obtained by faith. (God's ability to believe transferred into the heart of humanity).

In all this it revealed God was righteous in His actions and intentions. He acted justly to enable us to be justified.

To put it simply; the way in which God acts towards us, we can act towards Him.

Justification has been described in forensic terms as acquittal, opposed to condemnation; the releasing from the pain of blame.

Paul recognises his previous misguided lifestyle calling himself 'Chief of Sinners'
(1 Timothy 12:17 ESV)

He was a "wretched man" however he recognises that through being justified he was now free from his previous sinful ways. "I am what I am by the grace of God". Justification doesn't justify an old life with its sinful lusts and ways; it deals with the issues and then declares each free from the consequences of them. Through Christ, who served time in the correction centre of the Father's judgement, so, declaring us free from condemnation. We have not just been pardoned from the sin we committed we have been pardoned in fulfillment of the punishment that Jesus served for us. Sins are forgiven only because someone has already paid the penalty on our behalf.

We are declared just or righteous without denying the real righteousness of a person, simply, we do not qualify by our own merit, but by His sacrificial love.

By His knowledge my righteous servant shall justify many. For He shall bear their iniquities.

(Isaiah 53:11 ESV)

This prophetic description of Christ is simply describing the act of true redemption. It is His knowledge; He knows the way, truth and the life and His righteousness qualifies Him to justify many. He received, in His human flesh, the disfiguration of the consequences of sinful man.

He was wounded for our transgressions, bruised for our iniquities and the chastisement of our peace was upon Him, and by His stripes we are healed. (Isaiah 53:5 ESV)

It is only when one appreciates the cost and the consequences of the act of salvation that a true revelation of its effectiveness is seen. We do not receive additives or additions to our ordered life, we actually change our lifestyle to conform with His own - our life is hidden in Christ.

Our righteousness is as filthy rags, none are righteous no not one

(Romans 3:10 ESV)

Our righteousness disqualifies us from attempting an holistic well-being. It is therefore only His imputed righteousness that meets the ingredients for redemption.

Ravi Zacharias said, 'When you find your definitions in God, you find the very purpose for which you were created. Put your hand into God's hand; know His absolutes.'

Demonstrate His love, present His truth, and the message of redemption and transformation will take hold. Justification doesn't excuse or exonerate the sinful actions of humanity; it enables us to live a life free from the curse and penalty of those offences. We can justly face the future with our conviction of sin spent through Christ Jesus. It's not as people say "just as if I have never sinned". It is greater than that; it acknowledges that we have all sinned, yet we are no longer judged according to our guilt but the Saviour's righteousness. We are covered by His immunity. So, when death looks at us ready to devour, it sees Him who is the resurrection and the life. It seems that we have been transformed by the robe of righteousness into a clean, guiltless image of the Divine.

Humanity tries to justify position by logic and comparison, "I'm not as bad as them," or "I haven't done anybody any harm," or "I give to charity," or "I'm essentially a good person!"

They attempt to justify themselves by answering the questions they will not be asked! These are not the questions that the Almighty will be asking! He wants to know one thing:

"Have you been justified by My son Jesus Christ?"

The Apostle Paul could never have justified his behaviour in throwing men, women and children into prison because of their Christian faith. He could never justify his complicity to murder Stephen. He never tried to do it, "wretched man that I am". Yet after receiving justification by faith, he could legitimately say "I am what I am by His Grace". Guilt can never be submerged by grace unless a surrender of that guilt is given.

The titular hymn puts it: "take your burden to The Lord and leave it there"

Condemnation exists because we refuse to believe that the blood of Jesus Christ - God's own Son, cleanses us from all unrighteousness. True justification comes when the recipients are fully aware of their own lack of credibility; yet eagerly embrace the transforming love of Christ for us.

In the early 16th Century Luther had a third great experience. He was lecturing on the book of Psalms at the University of Wittenburg in 1513, then in 1515 on Romans, then in 1516 on Galatians. It was during these studies that Luther discovered a life transforming insight from the gospel - God's requirement, Sanctification and Holiness.

Sanctification is the act or process of acquiring sanctity or being made or becoming holy.

Bakers Evangelical Dictionary would simply say, "the state of proper functioning".

The description which is understandable is, "to set that person or thing apart for the use intended by its designer". The Greek word means, "holiness" – so these two words have an inseparable spiritual bond between them.

So, in the language of Christianity, sanctification is for our life and our gifting to be used as Christ intended. It obviously speaks of destiny and lifestyle, to achieve purpose and fulfillment in all aspects of our life and actions. As Christians we understand that we are commanded to both sanctify ourselves and be holy; this is both a process obtained by the Holy Spirit and a determined act of human will in refraining from those activities and actions that compromise our dedication to Christ and to the faith.

For I am the Lord your God. Consecrate yourselves therefore, and be holy, for I am holy. You shall not defile yourselves with any swarming thing that crawls on the ground (Leviticus 11:44 ESV)

This is an Old Testament command by God to consecrate or sanctify yourself and be holy. We could say in simple terms, 'have a good wash and stay away from the dirt, then commit yourself to being hygienic!'

The process is sensible:

We wash by His word, thus we become clean from the infections of a fallen world. We then, however, need to keep ourselves as much as possible from anything that would pollute our lives with compromise or sinful intent. We could, in simplistic description, refer to sanctification as a washing to reveal the purpose of our being, and holiness as setting ourselves apart to achieve these ideals.

By sanctifying yourself, it doesn't mean that we actually cleanse ourselves, however it does mean, like the prodigal son, that we must separate ourselves from the pig sty of compromise and submit to the washing of the Holy Spirit before keeping ourselves apart from the filth.

2 Thessalonians 2:13 is a defining scripture:

"He chose you to be saved through the sanctifying work of the spirit and through belief and truth."

It's the Holy Spirit that is the cleansing agent, but we need to stand under the shower of blessing. Sanctification is the process of being set apart and holiness is the progression of being set apart.

The Gospel of John, chapter seventeen, is one of the most challenging scriptures for me. This conversation with the Father is life-changing in its intensity. It's all about the Christian entering into a relationship of oneness with Christ - as He has with the Father.

In verse sixteen, Jesus speaking of the Christian says, "they are not of this world, just as I am not of this world". There is a noted separation from the governmental, cultural and spiritual authority of the believer. Verse seventeen then states, "Sanctify them in the truth, Your word is truth".

In paraphrase, Jesus is saying here, Father, as I am the Truth and I am the Word made flesh, wash them by the Word and separate them to yourself through and by me.

We are in Christ, Christ is in us, reconciling the world to the Father.

"We must hide our unholiness in the wounds of Christ as Moses hid himself in the cleft of the rock while the glory of God passed by... We must take refuge from God in God. Above all we must believe that God sees us perfect in His son while He disciplines and chastens and purges us that we may be partakers of His holiness." A.W.Tozer – "The Knowledge of the Holy" (page 107).

With the Jesus doctrine, it is simple yet profound; He is the source and the fulfillment of all we believe. We are called by His Name, The Christ, Christians, we are born of His name, saved by His blood, raised by His resurrection and interceded for by His actions and credibility.

C H Spurgeon put it beautifully,

"Our faith is a person; the gospel that we have to preach is a person; And go wherever we may, we have something solid and tangible to preach. For our gospel is a person. If you had asked the twelve Apostles in their day " what do you believe in?" they would not have stopped to go round about with a long sermon, but they would have pointed to their Master and said "we believe in Him" But what are your doctrines? "There they stand incarnate", But what is your practice?

"There stands our practice. He is our example." What then do you believe? Hear the glorious answer of the Apostles Paul, "We preach Christ crucified! Our Creed, our body of divinity, our whole theology is summed up in the person of Christ Jesus."

The Tabernacle in the desert and the Temple had this in common. The holiness of God was awesome; no person with sin in their lives could ever stand in the presence of the Almighty without being consumed by His integrity of holiness.

We, as mortals, could never hope to attain acceptability with God by human ingenuity or integrity, through the disobedience of one man, condemnation resulted for all men, yet through the act of righteousness of one man there resulted justification of life to all men.

Romans 5:19-20 tells how it was that act of a Holy God that resulted in humanity being reconciled to God through the righteous one [Jesus].

The High Priest in the Tabernacle and the Temple would once a year wash himself [sanctify] within the context of him being the forerunner of the Christ to come. The High Priest had garments that symbolised either the act of salvation or the qualities of the Christ to come. The garments included breeches to cover nakedness. God had to provide covering for Adam and Eve after they lost the covering of His righteousness. That is why, to a Christian, nakedness other than in the presence of one's husband or wife is revealing a fallen life rather than a covenanted relationship: Marriage, of course, solidifies that action.

A tunic of fine linen covered the whole body to the wrists; a sash and turban, together with a priestly blue robe including a fringe with golden bells and pomegranate, and tassels of blue, purple and scarlet.

The Ephod - a vest or apron embroidered with two onyx engraved gemstones on the shoulders with the names of the tribe of Israel, which carried the Urim and the Thummim.

The Breastplate with twelve gems bearing the names of the twelve tribes. On the front of the turban was a gold plate with the words, "Holiness unto YHWH".

The high Priest would not have shoes; like Moses he removed his shoes as a sign that his walk within the world had been left at the door. The washing and the bathing were a necessity before any robes could be applied.

It is not my desire to expound on each and every symbolic garment. It is, however, a reference to the elaborate conditions and symbolic nature of all the righteous requirements needed for intercession to be given for the sins of the people.

The High Priest would take the sacrificed lamb and cover himself with the sacrificial offering placing the blood on his ear lobe, thumb and big toe. The rest of the blood was sprinkled on the Mercy Seat on the top of the Ark of Covenant.

This should do two things for you; firstly bring a deeper understanding of what was needed to reconcile sinful humanity with a Holy God - every garment or object represented everything we had lost in relationship to the Almighty – yet, secondly, it revealed everything that Jesus was. The Great High Priest who manifested all these qualities embodied in human form wearing a Rabbi's gown with those same blue tassels.

This young man, living outside of the Holy of Holies, walking the streets and sitting with sinners yet still sanctified, not contaminated by the lustfulness of a fallen community.

There is little evidence of Jesus the carpenter; it is assumed that as Joseph was a carpenter that Jesus would follow in the business. However, when Jesus went missing he was found in the Temple listening to the Rabbi's debating and explaining the Law.

When challenged by His mother as to His actions He replied, "I must be about My Father's business". It is more likely that he was a Rabbi; He preached and read the scriptures in the Temple and sat in the preacher's chair - not normal for a carpenter!

It was those blue tassels that people all sought to touch for healing.

Mark tells us that within whichever town or region Jesus travelled they would place the sick in the market place and they would all cry out, "If we could just touch the hem of His garment..." and the many who did received healing - it was not just the woman who had the issue of blood.

The whole story of the High Priest and that of Jesus is unified in holiness. He may well have been anti-establishment and against legalism, yet He was still Holy in all His ways.

HOLINESS

It is, in essence, a reflection of what isn't. What do I mean? If there had never been sin, we would not have understood the reason for being set apart, to be sanctified. Clean people do not need washing. When Peter was rebuked by Jesus for not letting Him wash his feet Peter, totally misunderstanding what Jesus was saying, begged Jesus to wash him all over!

Jesus speaking of those sanctified by His presence said, "Peter you are already clean in spirit, it's your feet that smell!"

Isaiah reveals the benchmark of all holiness when he prophesied that seraphim call out to each other, "Holy, holy, holy is The Lord of hosts; the whole earth is full of His glory!" (Isaiah 6:3 ESV)

This is the concept of all that is separated from corruption, the pure focused character of the Almighty.

Holiness can cover a number of actions, including Godliness - perfecting His character within the lifestyle of the believer. To be "set apart" for service or for adoration.

In the Free Methodist Church that I serve, we have a strap line "Living Holiness" that has emerged from a time that the Church fell into intellectualism and legalism. It was full of rules, formulas and restrictive expectations.

The surrendering to the Holy Spirit [the clue is in the word Holy!] brings a freedom that, rather than killing the ability to be creative, promotes a living expectation of hope and fulfillment.

Our holiness is empowered by the desire to model ourselves on the thought "what would Jesus do?" not in a negative way but in a productive one.

The High Priest would enter the "Holy of Holies" once a year. This was set apart for the presence of God Almighty to dwell; the place of total surrender to the will of the Father in the expectation that His glory would descend upon the place.

Think for a moment - when there was holiness and sanctification the glory would fill the Tabernacle. When the priests kept not to their divisions but played and sang as one, the presence of The Lord filled the temple and they could no longer minister. When the disciples and other followers of Jesus came into a sanctified order, the fire descended as of tongues on every person.

The Tabernacle could be seen from the tents of the people.

The Temple could be felt on the pavement of the City.

The upper room could be heard by the masses in Jerusalem.

True holiness is not categorically monastic in its piety; it can be seen in the drunken noise of the upper room when the people mistakenly thought that these hallowed people had been drinking rather than being filled with the Holy Spirit. It can be seen in the breaking of bread house to house.

Just as in the Wesley holiness meetings where often depraved foul-mouthed individuals found themselves paralysed by the convicting power of the Holy Spirit true holiness, rather than isolating the recipient from his or her community, attracts the community to them - holiness is magnetic in its manifestation.

For it was indeed fitting that we should have such a high priest, holy, innocent, unstained, separated from sinners, and exalted above the heavens. He has no need, like those high priests, to offer sacrifices daily, first for his own sins and then for those of the people, since he did this once for all when he offered up himself. For the law appoints men in their weakness as high priests, but the word of the oath, which came later than the law, appoints a Son who has been made perfect forever. (Hebrews 7:26-28 ESV)

One would assume that Christ Jesus who qualified for all these qualities would be unapproachable, "separate from sinners" yet the contradiction is seen in Mark 2 - the religious leaders ask a question, "Why does He eat with tax collectors and sinners?" if He is separate from sinners, Why?

Because He was IN the world but not OF its values.

In John 17, Jesus asks that we Christians should not be taken out of this world, but rather that the world be taken out of us.

You can be friends of, and with, sinners without being affected with their dysfunction.

People loved Jesus and found Him receptive when those of religious philosophy were dismissive of them.

Religion means "to bind together" and for those who have no concept of pure religion which is, according to Paul, to feed the poor and to care for the widows and orphans, it is a lifeless, legalistic set of expectations approved of man and then accredited to God!

As Christians we can live among unbelievers without assimilating their lifestyle or values - holding firm to the tenets of faith.

Holiness is not a passive lifeless attribute but a fervent experience. It's the fervent prayer of the righteous that avails much or is powerful and effective, produces wonderful results, or can accomplish much - James 5:16

Passivity is not the model for righteous holy living, we are called to fight the good fight of faith!

Fight the good fight of the faith. Take hold of the eternal life to which you were called and about which you made the good confession in the presence of many witnesses. (1 Timothy 6:12 ESV)

"Take hold of eternal life" having first taken on the "good fight of faith"

JC Ryle said that:

"Necessity is laid upon us. We must fight. There are no promises in The Lord Jesus Christ's epistles to the seven churches, except to those who 'overcome". Where there is grace, there will be conflict. The believer is a soldier. There is no holiness without warfare. Saved souls will always be found to have fought a fight "

Our holiness is not to be practiced within the walls of a sanctuary alone, but in the highways of all our communities.

Pope Benedictine XVI observed:

"How much we need, in the Church and in society, witnesses of the beauty of holiness, witnesses of the splendour of truth, witnesses of the joy and freedom born of a living relationship with Christ"

It's that authenticity of normal sacred living that personifies the actions of Christians. It isn't the two extremes of either worldliness or exclusion from society.

It's touching the sinner without sinning, the sick without becoming ill.

It's asking people to catch your health and wholeness!

Paul speaks of the Jesus doctrine of not being "unequally yoked" together with unbelievers, for what fellowship has righteousness with lawlessness? And what communion has light with darkness? And what accord has Christ with Belial (the wicked or worthless)? Or what part has a believer with an unbeliever? And what agreement has the temple of God with idols?

For we are the temple of the living God; as God said,

"I will make my dwelling among them and walk among them, and I will be their God, and they shall be my people". (2 Corinthians 6:16 ESV)

Paul deals with this with a number of illustrations:

[1] He contrasts Christians as righteous people who have experienced personal forgiveness and who are pursuing the purposes of God. He then compares those with who he calls lawless. This doesn't suggest that people who don't yet submit to Christ are either rebels or criminals - it is better translated as those who do not live by the laws of God, so becoming "lawless". He speaks of fellowship. The partnership of soul "Koinonia" the closest of all fellowship, especially with people who share one's interests.

[2] He then contrasts communion - the sharing or exchanging of intimate thoughts and feelings, especially on a spiritual level of light and darkness, the answer of course is it can't happen. Light will always drive darkness away.

[3] He then brings accord into the discussion. To grant someone power, status, recognition.

The question is why would Christ give Belial or simply the demonic this status?

[4] He then simply spells it out what part - an amount or section which, when combined with others, makes up the whole of something - has a believer with an unbeliever? Basically, would you consider forming a whole relationship with those who have no common interest in the Almighty?

[5] He finishes with what agreement - harmony or accordance in

opinion or feeling - between the Temple and Idols. The contrast is stark; the house of God should not be infiltrated by the gods of this world. Agreement is the merging of two people or more in a way of action or purpose.

So, Paul makes it perfectly clear that our righteousness and holiness are often offered in compromise, our need and desire for fellowship, communion, accord, to be part of, an agreement with others can leave us vulnerable to compromise.

The richness of our relationship with Jesus Christ leaves us open to seduction and abduction. Great leaders have fallen because of either their ministry being seduced or abducted - self becomes the centre of worship.

Paul uses the analogy of the day, oxen being harnessed in the stock totally different in size, temperament and purpose. The people of his day understood that it would either never happen, or it would never work.

There was a barbaric punishment in the days of old. A man found guilty of a crime could have a dead person chained to them. As the body started to decompose the disease would gradually eat into the living subject so bringing death to the recipient. To carry around a dead body was both disgraceful and disruptive and, eventually, the bringer of death. it made a statement to the community.

When we are "tethered" to those who are dead in sin, we face the similar emotional and spiritual degeneration.

It is for discipline that you have to endure. God is treating you as sons. For what son is there whom his father does not discipline? If you are left without discipline, in which all have participated, then you are illegitimate children and not sons. Besides this, we have had earthly fathers who disciplined us, and we respected them. Shall we not much more be subject to the Father of spirits and live? For they disciplined us for a short time as it seemed best to them, but he disciplines us for our good, that we may share his holiness. For the moment all discipline seems painful rather than pleasant, but later it yields the peaceful fruit of righteousness to those who have been trained by it. (Hebrews 12:7-14 ESV)

Therefore, lift your drooping hands and strengthen your weak knees, and make straight paths for your feet, so that what is lame may not be put out of joint but rather be healed. Strive for peace with everyone, and for the holiness without which no one will see the Lord.

The writer sees holiness as so important that he likens it to being implanted into the lifestyle by a father bringing discipline to a child. That word "chasten" means to educate or discipline and instruct. It speaks of teaching and expecting a learning process to take place. So, holiness is not an instantaneous experience, but an on-going expectation for every believer.

Strive for peace with everyone, and for the holiness without which no one will see the Lord. See to it that no one fails to obtain the grace of God; that no "root of bitterness" springs up and causes trouble, and by it many become defiled; that no one is sexually immoral or unholy like Esau, who sold his birth right for a single meal. For you know that afterward, when he desired to inherit the blessing, he was rejected, for he found no chance to repent, though he sought it with tears. (Hebrews 12:14-17 ESV)

The writer speaks of pursuing peace with all people; that is not a call for compromise but for the desire to reconcile through love and forgiveness that leads to peace with God and the peace of God. Then we pursue holiness, why? Because unless we are separated from the "flesh" we can't even see God - what can rob us of this oneness with the Father?

Root of bitterness

A situation that has not been fully resolved leaves a seed of resentment and disfiguration. Many become defiled. This can lead to moral decline and a perverse and profane lifestyle.

It cites Esau who, having sold his birth right for a "mess of pottage' or, as I say, "a potted message!" could find no reconciliation even with many tears.

True Christianity is a combination of God approaching man and man responding to God. We cannot engage with God unless or until the Holy Spirit first convicts, reveals the magnitude of God to us and the sinfulness of the human soul.

It's through this conviction of Sin, His Righteousness and the reality that we must all stand before the judgment seat of God that brings us into a position of response. We have to activate that faith by our confession. If we confess our sins He is faithful and just to forgive us our sins.

We have a responsive faith. He loved us, we love Him. He forgave us, we forgive others.

He said, "follow Me" we do. He said, "Go into all the world and make disciples of every nation" and we have.

Jesus said, "lay hands on the sick and they will recover" We do, and they do.

GRACE – FAVOUR OR GOODWILL

For by grace you have been saved through faith. And this is not your own doing; it is the gift of God, not a result of works, so that no one may boast. (Ephesians 2:8-9 ESV)

Paul is saying that we are made righteous by the favour of God, not by human effort. It is indicative of a generous God that He bestows on the human soul favours beyond imagination.

Paul shares what seems controversial to many, his "thorn in his flesh":

Now to each one the manifestation of the Spirit is given for the common good. To one there is given through the Spirit a message of wisdom, to another a message of knowledge by means of the same Spirit, to another faith by the same Spirit, to another gifts of healing by that one Spirit, to another miraculous powers, to another prophecy, to another distinguishing between spirits, to another speaking in different kinds of tongues, and to still another the interpretation of tongues. (1 Corinthians 12:6-7 NIV)

Many will argue that this thorn was not a physical imperfection, but a spiritual testing, however we know it was an invasion of the flesh. He becomes provocative by stating that this challenge came because there was a possibility of him becoming conceited - why? Because he moved in incredible revelations. Paul realised that he was so used of God there was a real possibility that he would start believing his own publicity! It was not sent from God, it was however allowed as it was through the protective screen by a messenger of Satan.

Paul did not accept this invasion with a submissive attitude, three times he pleaded - actually begged - for God to intervene. Paul was desperate, yet the only answer he received was "My Grace is sufficient for you" the power of God is made perfect in the weakness of man. What a revelation, when man is at his weakest, God reveals the fullness of His power.

Paul therefore boasts in his weakness; not promoting his deficiencies, but rather revealing that the power that becomes obvious in his life is accredited to Christ alone. The thorn is debatable. I personally believe it was his eyes.

Where, then, is your blessing of me now? I can testify that, if you could have done so, you would have torn out your eyes and given them to me. (Galatians 4:15 NIV)

In verse 13 Paul confirms that he suffered "bodily ailment"

He confirms that his condition was at first a great trial to the Galatians - but you received me -

He said, "If it was possible, you would have gouged out your eyes and given them to me".

Paul may have used others to write his letters for other reasons, or it may have been his difficulty with sight. Tetris wrote down the book of Romans adding his own greeting. Paul often added a piece to letters 1 Corinthians 16:21, 2 Thessalonians 3:17, Galatians 6:11 even records Paul as saying that he had written in "his own large hand". The actual "thorn" may never be known to us, I wouldn't want my readers to spend time arguing over the condition but rather concentrating on the power of God's Grace that enabled Paul to not only maintain his ministry, but to become the cornerstone of faith. This enabled him to reject "believing his own publicity"! It reveals the character of the man when he could publicly share his vulnerability; Grace (God's favour) totally neutralised the debilitating effects of the affliction.

What Satan meant for harm, God used for good.

Wikipedia describes Grace as "a theological term; it has been defined as the Divine influence which operates in humans to regenerate and sanctify, to inspire virtuous impulses, and to impart strength to endure trial and resist temptation".

[1] A Divine influence

It gives the impression of us having a friend in high places! One who can pull strings or put in a word for us. And, of course, that is Jesus, who lives to make intercession for us (Hebrews 7:24-25 ESV).

[2] Inspire virtuous impulses

Rather than overreact and become impulsive and irrational in our actions and attitudes to life, He brings the inspiration by his favour so that we react impulsively by Grace, so endeavouring to keep the bond of peace.

[3] To impart strength to endure trial and to resist temptation

These three give us the credibility needed for a victorious life, as we are strengthened in the inner man, we will face hardship and trial. His Grace will enable us to endure hardship as a good soldier.

It is important to note that the first Adam submitted to temptation, Yet the second Adam [Jesus] resisted temptation. Grace, therefore, gives us the divinely inspired courage and determination to resist and to overcome the strategy of the fallen angel.

Jesus modelled a prayer for His disciples that included, "lead me not into temptation but deliver me from evil". It is His Grace that enables us to walk away from the rigours of deception.

What causes quarrels and what causes fights among you? Is it not this, that your passions are at war within you? You desire and do not have, so you murder. You covet and cannot obtain, so you fight and quarrel. You do not have, because you do not ask. You ask and do not receive, because you ask wrongly, to spend it on your passions. You adulterous people! Do you not know that friendship with the world is enmity with God? Therefore, whoever wishes to be a friend of the world makes himself an enemy of God. Or do you suppose it is to no purpose that the Scripture says, "He yearns jealously over the spirit that he has made to dwell in us"? But he gives more grace. Therefore, it says, "God opposes the proud but gives grace to the humble."

(James 4:1-6 ESV)

James is identifying the cause of friction among people; we often ask of God but never receive - why? It's because of wrong motives.

James is very strong in his description of those who share the values of this world, he calls them adulterers, "friendship with the world makes one an enemy of God." That is very strong in its context. What's the answer? More grace.

God opposes the proud but gives grace to the humble.

I'm somewhat disturbed by many who have, through ignorance, relabelled grace as the "get out of jail free" card.

When sinning, l hear them say, "I'm living in grace not law"!

Grace actually empowers us to live above the demand of the law.

Romans 6 is so clear:

"What shall we say to all this?"

Are we to remain in sin in order that God's grace may overflow? Certainly Not! How can we who died to sin live in it any longer? Grace rather than excusing sin gives the ability to overcome temptation. Jesus explains the difference between law and grace; law says "don't commit adultery", Grace says "don't even lust after them".

Law says, "don't kill" Grace says "don't be angry with your brother". Rather than grace being softer, it is actually living at a higher expectation.

We need to teach a correct understanding of grace and its significance within the life believer in Christ Jesus.

Grace in the Old Testament sees the children of Israel being liberated from Egypt and then being established in the Promised Land. The New Testament sees the humanity liberated from sin and established in Righteousness.

Billy Graham said:

"If it weren't for God's grace, you and I wouldn't be able to live for even one minute. God's grace sustains us every moment of the day and without His grace we couldn't even exist. We think we have control of our lives - but if it weren't for God's grace we wouldn't even be alive"

Rt Revd J C Ryle, the first Bishop of Liverpool, said about grace:

"My chief desire in all my writings, is to exalt The Lord Jesus Christ and make Him beautiful and glorious in the eyes of men; and to promote the increase of repentance, faith and holiness upon earth"

John Bunyan Writer of "Pilgrims Progress" wrote a complete book addressing the subject of grace called "Grace Abounding to the Chief of Sinners "

As a minister within the world Methodist group, I long to see the impact of our previous historic outpouring on the spiritual climate today; the grace of God was a daily experience translated into social and spiritual reformation. Many historians believe that England was on the verge of civil war at the time of the French Revolution. It was the preaching of His Grace from the Wesley brothers that turned the nation to seek God.

The Church blending its traditions would see the means of grace being manifested through the preached word, baptism, Eucharist and among the traditional wing of the church confession, as a way of maintaining the value of His Grace

The Augsburg Confession

The Lutheran Reformation 1530

Describes the outworking of the means of grace as "The Church is a congregation of saints, in which the Gospel is rightly taught, and the sacraments are rightly administered"

Nelson's Commentary would associate grace with mercy, love, compassion, patience. We could say that grace attracts like attributes, it's the link whereby these other Christ-like qualities flow.

Therefore, preparing your minds for action, and being sober-minded, set your hope fully on the grace that will be brought to you at the revelation of Jesus Christ. (1 Peter 1: 13 ESV)

Peter challenges the reader to "prepare their minds for action" to be sober or don't be flippant! In the hope [deferred reality] of His grace being revealed by Christ Jesus.

So, we are seeing a pattern emerging; grace not only brings us to Salvation, it leads us onward into Salvation. In one sense grace is the motivational force that maintains and encourages the believer on the upward journey.

John Wesley's teaching involved means and works of Grace.

He taught that God's grace is unearned and that we were not to be idle waiting to experience grace, but we are to engage in the means of grace. The means of Grace are the ways God works invisibly in His disciples.

Works of Piety

Reading, meditating and studying scriptures, prayer, fasting, regularly attending worship, healthy living and sharing our faith with others.

Communal Practices

Regularly share the sacraments, Christian conferencing, [accountability to one another] and bible study.

Work of mercy

Doing good works, visiting the sick, those in prison, feeding the hungry, and giving generously to the needs of others.

Community Practices

Seeking justice, ending oppression and discrimination [ending slavery in his day] and addressing the needs of the poor.

This he believed would grow both disciples and congregations.

It makes one wonder if these practices, if implemented into the present Churches would receive the same results as he saw!

"Do not keep a record or an account of your work, give up being book-keeper. In the Christian life we must desire nothing but His glory, nothing but to please Him. So, do not keep your eye on the clock, but keep it on Him and His work" Dr. Martyn Lloyd-Jones in his sermon "All by Grace".

These preachers are basically saying, it's all about Christ not me. He favoured us by His grace, we found a way out of death and hell by grace, we maintain our spiritual walk by grace. We are healed by His grace, we are prepared for eternity by His grace. Do you receive the message?

The divine interaction with the human soul leaves us in no doubt that our salvation was not contrived but intentional.

So, as we come to the end of Grace how do we leave it for each one of us to live truly in the grace of God?

Submit yourselves, then, to God. Resist the devil, and he will flee from you (James 4:7 NIV)

[1] Submit yourselves then to God

That is not easy for any of us, submission firstly must be voluntary. I can't pray, "Lord submit for me"! It has to be my choice. Submission through grace is not slavery, it's true sonship and servanthood to the Lord. It's freedom to hand over our personal agenda on the understanding that He never abuses our trust or vulnerability.

[2] Resist the devil

That word resist is not passive, it's offensive, placing obstacles in the path of the enemy, not allowing his devious aspirations of fallen humanity to become the norm in the lives of the believer.

We overcome [resist] by the blood of the Lamb and the word of our testimony.

[3] And he will flee from you

James doesn't say "he will leave you alone" he says "flee" - the concept of speed and flight; the swiftness of our deliverance comes by submission to the purposes of God and the resistance to the pollution of Satan.

Grace is often used as a template for those who diligently suppress the works of the flesh, or simply those desires or thoughts that war against the purposes of God for our lives.

Holy Communion

There is no single, appropriate way of celebrating communion. In contradiction to your Church tradition, there is no correct method of either preparing or distributing the bread and wine, other than having taken notice of Paul's warning to examine our hearts and motives; not to eat of the bread nor drink of the cup in an unworthy manner (1 Corinthians 11:27 NKJV).

Communion is ordered according to traditions and these vary in their presentation, delivery and enaction. It is the responsibility of the communicant to be right with the Lord, in preparation for the celebration. It is not for the preacher, priest, pastor or leader to conduct the ceremony in a particular manner.

The description or methodology of the act is of little importance; it's the reality of the act that infuses the communicant with the sacrificial love of the Lamb, slain before the foundation of the world. It is the examination of oneself that is vital in our appreciation of an ongoing need to be righteous in our relationship with both God and man.

The Traditions

The Jewish church, born out of the Day of Pentecost, was modelling the traditional Jewish cultural aspect of 'breaking bread'. As the Church was integrated with Gentiles, this evolved.

The Roman/ Orthodox theology offers a Christian mystical aspect to the Eucharist. This includes the way the bread is prepared and delivered; regimented by a belief in the mystical transformation of the elements. In the Reformation, there evolved a less ritualistic delivery of the 'Communion'.

The main difference between the Catholic and the Protestant Churches is the doctrine of Transubstantiation. The traditional belief is that the bread and wine used in the sacrament of the Eucharist become not merely a sign or figure, but also in reality the body and the blood of Christ.

This has not only become a theological problem between the strands of Christendom but has historically produced martyrs on both sides. The Protestants are diversified in their beliefs from near transubstantiation to a simple identity based in some bread and a sip of wine.

The trend of the modern Charismatic Church, with its desire to become culturally identified with the visitor, is often to discreetly move its celebration to a less visible time in the church's diary, or only to celebrate on special occasions. With the traditional liturgical denominations, the communion is the central experience, with other expressions even the lessons basically emerge from this.

I often find that true balance is nearer the centre of the debate rather than at either of the two extremes.

My Pentecostal upbringing saw it as a Sunday morning experience when only Christians normally ventured into the building. It was generally thought that non-Christians needed their own 'experience' on a Sunday evening! We believed it was a symbol and we would celebrate it as a new wave Passover meal; blackcurrant cordial with sliced bread pulled into small cubes.

Yet, even as pure symbolism, we still treated the service with respect; believing that if a non-believer ever indulged, they could or would drop dead or face the wrath of God in this life or the next!

Even as non-conformists we stood in a circle around a table that had a white cover over the elements. A Pastor or Elder would pray a prayer of thanksgiving for the undying love of Christ for His sacrifice. Then either in quietness or with the piano or organ playing, the communion tray with little glasses upon it would be passed down the pews. Before this happened, the Pastor or delegated leaders would make it clear to all that if you had not found Christ, you would probably be consumed with fire should you accidentally participate!

The command of Christ at the last Passover meal was to "do this in remembrance of Me till I come". (1 Corinthians 11: 24-26)

And when He (Jesus) had given thanks, He broke it and said, "This is my body, which is for you; do this in remembrance of Me". In the same way, He took the cup also after supper, saying, "This cup is the new covenant in My blood; do this, as often as you drink it, in remembrance of Me. For as often as you eat this bread and drink this cup you proclaim The Lord's death until He comes".

The difference in the theology is that the Catholic thought is literal; that as Jesus said, "this is my body and my blood", it miraculously changes at the point of consumption.

The Protestant view is that Jesus foretelling his death was engaging a new Passover meal that celebrated His sacrifice without the re-crucifying of His flesh

For Christ also suffered once for sins, the righteous for the unrighteous, that He might bring us to God, being put to death in the flesh but made alive in the spirit. (1 Peter 3:18 ESV)

On this premise they cannot agree with the veneration of the emblems as His body. However, if we look at the other extreme thought amongst non-conformists, it can become flippant and even disrespectful. In the Anglican, Roman Catholic and Orthodox traditions the whole service is centered round the communion. Pentecostal and Evangelical Christians would choose to centralise the preaching of the Word or even in some Churches, the expression of Worship.

As we look more closely into the very act of the Communion we see the message of covenant, or as Jesus puts it, "a new covenant" an agreement between God and His people, in which God makes promises to His people and, usually, requires certain conduct from them in return. In the Old Testament, God made such agreements with Noah and Abraham.

As Christ sets this second 'Passover", death would not visit those who carried the blood; not of a literal lamb upon a door mantle but of the Lamb of God whose blood covers all who truly repent of sin.

Death came in Egypt to all who refused to embrace the covering of the blood offering. So, within the new covenant there is danger for those who take it in an unworthy manner.

Therefore, whoever eats the bread or drinks the cup of The Lord in an unworthy manner, shall be guilty of the body and the blood of The Lord. But a man must examine himself, and in so he is to eat of the bread and drink of the cup. For He who eats and drinks, eats and drinks judgment to himself if he does not judge the body rightly. For this reason, many among you are weak and sick, and a number sleep. (1 Corinthians 11:27-30 NASB1995

So, we see that the partaking of the Communion has serious consequences to those who do not take it with righteous conduct. It is a revisiting of the first Passover calamity, the death of the first born. So, one would have to say that it's more than symbolism. But again, as I have repeated throughout this book – it is not the act itself but the THOUGHT that predicates it. Is there a 'right-thought' – a preparation of the inner person, a righteousness within God, that prepares each of us to take communion? It is this that is the imperative – not the style, tone, method or delivery. I expect each expression of communion to be treated with reverence. But I don't reject any expression based on its theatre – I challenge each person to examine themselves even as they prepare to take communion. 1 Corinthians 11:27-30 is very clear on this.

As the Apostolic leader of the Order of St Leonard, I have led our development in the spirit of Oneness – holding fast to that which unites us as Christians. This means that we are a convergence Order, enabling the Liturgical, Sacramental, Evangelical and Charismatic to live in harmony with one other. We do not determine the formation of the elements, nor do we seek to modify the act to conform with one tradition; indeed, in the presence of any of these four Christian expressions, we will celebrate according to that tradition. This is the beauty of the Order! We embrace the traditions of the wide Church family, but we do not dictate them.

This very act of unity and Oneness has exposed bigotry, legalism, flippancy and intolerance; this should not be brethren!

Whatever your Christian tradition, if you find the crucified and risen Christ in your formation, wonderful. However, I caution against allowing the diversity of method to isolate you from you fellow Christians. Known differently within all the denominations as The Mass, Breaking of Bread, Eucharist, The Lord's Table and the Lord's Supper, this book does not seek to examine the varied doctrinal arguments that have separated the Church, that have validated structure over substance and legalism over righteousness. My aim, only, is to demonstrate that which unites us and, in the case of Holy Communion, to reinforce the validity of the act itself and the examination of self that is unique to each individual.

The bread was left in the presence of The Lord for one week and then because it had been in His presence, only Priests could eat it. (Exodus 25:30)

Let us now work this through. Bread absorbs the taste and flavour of that which it is exposed to.

For example, in the presence of smoke or perfume it will taste of that. It doesn't become that object, yet it tastes of it. So, if the bread is in the presence of Almighty God, then the children of Israel truly believed that it absorbed His presence - not His body. When we bring our communion to Christ, we all ask Him to bless it with His presence. Therefore, only those who have been cleansed by the shedding of His blood are priests unto Him and should eat of that bread.

When I considered this, it changed my attitude to these precious emblems, not transubstantiation, but a form of real presence.

This is a releasing, powerful thought; this bread and cup being offered to His presence gives a true understanding of the act of Calvary. The Communion, therefore, regardless of its style or presentation, should be sacred in its application. Few other actions can result in some becoming sick, and others prematurely dying!

RESTITUTION

This is a teaching of Christ that is seldom addressed in modern theology. Often people are told that when they commit their lives to Christ, their past life, with all its imperfections, is totally exonerated.

The answer is yes, we are forgiven and made new in Christ Jesus, yet the consequences of our old life remain to be addressed.

Becoming a Christian does not negate our responsibility for past actions that still have present unfinished issues.

We see a classic story of this when the Apostle Paul writes a letter to Philemon a church leader in Colossi; it's about Onesimus – a runaway slave. His name means beneficial or useful - there is power in a name! This slave was of value, even if he did not know it.

We may have been slaves to many things during our life yet when we become Christians, the bible tells us that we are given a new name known only to him.

One thing I know, it's meaning will epitomise the destiny of our life!

When Paul is in prison, we don't know the circumstances that brought him into contact with Onesimus; but we do know that as a slave, Onesimus would have met with Paul during his visits to Philemon.

We gather that Onesimus had run away from his home and could have stolen money during that act. He commits his life to Christ; he can now live in the potential of his name and he becomes a close friend of Paul, yet he is not legally free. Paul, understanding the law, knows that if Onesimus is ever detained by the authorities, he will be arrested and will suffer detention for life.

Paul knows that Onesimus will never be free until he returns to Philemon and deals with his past.

Paul offers to mediate between them, as he genuinely loves these two Christians.

Paul understands the difficulty involved in forgiveness and restitution - he fell out with Barnabas over his relative John Mark. Paul seeing the indifference of John Mark is angry when he prematurely leaves the Apostles and returns home. The fallout split these two friends, yet Paul reconciled the situation, now having John Mark on his team.

If you have not overcome your own past issues, you have no credibility to intervene in anyone's issues.

Paul is willing to support Onesimus, yet he must go back!

Paul as a free man became a prisoner for the truth.

Onesimus, a prisoner, could become a free man through the same truth.

The truth put Paul into captivity; the truth would take Onesimus out of the captivity of slavery.

There is a teaching that has damaged the development of many Christians; it is simply the misinterpreting of our personal responsibilities after conversion. Most people are taught that the cross not only forgives your past, it negates any personal responsibility for the past. Yet the bible clearly teaches restitution.

Paul is saying clearly, "Onesimus, you need to return to Philemon regardless of the consequences and face up to your responsibilities, you are now a free man, act like it!"

We don't know what happened after the return, however we see in Colossians 4:8-10 that Paul sends Tychicus to the Church at Colossi with Onesimus, "a faithful and beloved brother who is one of you".

We assume that Philemon releases him to be a free man.

Today we need to ask some serious questions as to our past, not ones of condemnation but of accountability. As Christians we need to know that we now have the ability and the responsibility to address the outstanding issues that we may not have confronted until today.

Zacchaeus was a classic example of what Onesimus was to do.

Luke 19 tells us the story of this man, small in stature, climbing a tree to see Jesus in the midst of the crowd. Jesus stops, and looks up, calls him by name, and invites Himself to tea.

We know nothing of the conversation, it's private, we can't even speculate. The meeting now ends and as Jesus walks down the pathway, Zacchaeus is heard to say, "Look, Lord, I give half of my goods to feed the poor [Grace] and if I have taken anything from anyone by false accusation, I restore fourfold [Law]".

Giving back fourfold is part of the Jewish law; for all who needed to make restitution. In simple terms, if he had stolen 15,000 he would have paid back 60,000 – the law expected it.

Yet through meeting Jesus he goes further into Grace: "Half of my goods to feed the poor"

Jesus now speaks to him saying, "Today salvation has come this house".

This is the only time in the bible that Jesus uses such language before the cross. What is He saying? Dealing with the past clears the deck; the enemy cannot restrict one's future.

Charles Wesley aptly put in his hymn – "And can it be that I should gain":
"Long my imprisoned spirit lay,
Fast bound in sin and nature's night
Thine eye diffused a quickening ray
I woke; the dungeon flamed with light;
My chains fell off; my heart was free.
I rose went forth and followed thee".

The next verse starts with "No condemnation now I dread; Jesus and all in Him is mine"

If you are a thief, quit stealing - instead, use your hands for good hard work and then give generously to others in need. (Ephesians 4:28 NLT)

The woman at the well, basically sexually immoral she was transformed by the words of Christ.
"Out of your belly shall flow rivers of living water, you will never thirst again"
What did she do? She left her bucket and immediately visited the men of the town (the women had ostracised her!)
Interesting, five husbands lost, now living with a man and not married to him, and then calling on men to come and see Jesus.
This defied all cultural protocol. She was pleading with these men to come and listen to Jesus - the one who could transform their lives.
They could immediately see the difference in her. They all came to see Him. As they surrendered their lives to Him they said, "We first believed because of her, we now believe as we have met you

for ourselves".

Our issues may not be previous sin or wrongdoing. We may have to revisit wrong decisions;

Elisha was chosen to follow Elijah, yet when called he couldn't leave his family or his business.

Elijah replied to him "what have I to do with you?"

In simple terms, if you don't want to be used just say so!

Elisha had to return home and deal with the things in his past that were stopping him securing his future.

So, be you like Onesimus, Zaachaeus, the women at the well or Elisha - or be you who you are - are there any outstanding issues?

You may have made wrong decisions, maybe you walked away from responsibilities or children or families - financial commitments - it doesn't mean you can turn the clock back, it does mean you can make amends.

A letter or phone call of apology if a personal meeting is not possible; the support of a child you fathered and then walked away, or were driven away, from. What about the old person you robbed, or the person you gossiped about?

Or are you still a slave of yesterday's mistakes?

Come with Onesimus today and be free from the past once and for all time.

Rick Warren said:

"We are products of our past, but we don't have to be prisoners of it".

So true. We can be free.

Oscar Wilde said:

"No man is rich enough to buy back his past"

That is also true, however I know a man who has done that for me, The Lord Jesus Christ!

Restitution is not purchasing forgiveness, it's the opposite, it's the realisation that our past has been redeemed not with silver or gold, but with the precious blood of Christ.

Now, if He purchased my salvation with His life, l can face up to the outstanding injustices that l have left unattended.

This is obviously a theological dilemma to those who desire to walk from the consequences of our actions. There is a difference between forgiveness and restitution.

Forgiveness is God forgiving us for our action of sin, Restitution is our response to that forgiveness by restoring with interest.

God forgives the violation that disables us from walking in His path of righteousness, yet our desire must always be to make recompense to those who are true victims of our dysfunctional ways.

The way we face the responsibilities of our past will determine the magnitude of our future.

The Apostle Paul's past of violence and complicity was not easily rectified, yet he became reconciled by the servant spirit.

The Judgment Seat of God

Twenty-first century Christianity has, in many Churches, disowned any reference to personal accountability to God after the death of the believer.

But...

...we must all appear before the judgment seat of Christ, so that each may receive what is due for what he has done in the body, whether good or evil. (2 Corinthians 5:10 ESV)

You, then, why do you judge your brother or sister? Or why do you treat them with contempt? For we will all stand before God's judgement seat. (Romans 14:10 ESV)

The theological fallout in the timing, place, sequences and who this affects has robbed many preachers of the confidence to preach this biblical truth!

Will each individual personally stand amidst billions to give an account, or collectively stand before the omnipresence of the Holy Spirit who can search both the heart and memory file of each and every one in a blink of the eye?

Is this the defining moment of heaven or hell?

Is it just for saints or is it exclusively for sinners?

What are the differences between the Judgment seat of Christ and the Great White Throne?

We could write a book just examining the differing theological interpretations on who, what, when and why. The only message I wish to share is there is a time of accountability that we must all attend.

Just as people are destined to die once, and after that to face judgment. (Hebrews 9:27 NIV)

According to the grace of God given to me, like a skilled master builder I laid a foundation, and someone else is building upon it. Let each one take care how he builds upon it. For no one can lay a foundation other than that which is laid, which is Jesus Christ. Now if anyone builds on the foundation with gold, silver, precious stones, wood, hay, straw— each one's work will become manifest, for the Day will disclose it, because it will be revealed by fire, and the fire will test what sort of work each one has done. If the work that anyone has built on the foundation survives, he will receive a reward. If anyone's work is burned up, he will suffer loss, though he himself will be saved, but only as through fire. (1 Corinthians 3:10-15 ESV)

In this passage Paul is describing that the Gospel had been preached and the doctrines delivered by many Apostolic leaders Paul planted and Apollos watered, but God Himself brought the increase.

Paul then speaks of the reward that each individual will receive according to their personal gifting and obedience.

Christ being the foundation of our faith we build, Paul gives the material that Christians often use to build on Christ: gold, silver, precious stones, wood, hay, straw.

Verse 13

Each one's work will become clear; for the Day will declare it, because it will be revealed by fire; and the fire will test each one's work, of what sort it is.

Verse 14

If anyone's work which he has built on endures, he will receive a reward.

Verse 15

If anyone's work is burned, he will suffer loss;

but he himself will be saved, yet so as through fire.

We are commanded to lay up treasure in heaven where thief or rust or moth cannot have access.

Even with scriptural evidence, many in the evangelical wing of the Church are being influenced by humanistic and pluralistic thinking.

In a graphical description Paul clearly reveals that what we build our Christian life with must face the testing of the Holy Spirit - gold, silver and precious stones actually become more valuable through the process of heat.

The imperfections are released from the objects leaving a purity of metal - when cooled they become of greater value.

However, wood, and hay are combustible, and stone has no increasing value, most of these are consumed by heat as they have no substance.

We can build our life with spiritual materials that have little or no eternal qualities.

So, what is Paul saying? Eternal life is not just our qualification for heaven, we carry valuable assets into the presence of the

Almighty. These assets are obviously needed for our position and function. The prodigal son is a classic example of one who built with combustible materials. He was saved on his return, however retaining nothing of his inheritance. When his brother complained, thinking he would receive a second inheritance, his father said " No!" then he said

"look around you and see all this land, it's yours".

Eternal life is not eternal cloud-sitting, learning the harp!

There will be a new heaven and new earth – there will be functioning people. Adam and Eve inherited the creational substance from the breath of the Almighty.

God cannot deny his nature, we are not created to be celestial cloud-loungers!

We are rulers, overseers, we are a creative creation.

According to your eschatology, we may rule with Him for one thousand years on the earth!

It's going to be a hard day's night! [There is no night in heaven!]

2 Corinthians v3 is written to believers, "Unto the church of God which is at Corinth"...Paul again reiterates "we must all appear before the judgment seat of Christ".

Revelation 20 speaks about the "Great White Throne".

This dramatically speaks of the sea and the earth giving up their dead. It's all about being found or not in the Lamb's book of life. John vividly describes that whoever is not found in the book of life was cast into the lake of fire. Theologians have not all agreed on the geography or the literal expression of this lake, however John is leaving the reader in no doubt that there is a dividing of what Matthew calls the "sheep and the goats" in Chapter 25.

Jesus in the parable of the wise and the foolish virgins speaks clearly about a wedding feast, the invited guests fell asleep, or, in our language, were spiritually waiting for the Day of The Lord.

At the cry "Behold the bridegroom is coming, go out to meet Him" the wise entered the feast and the door is firmly shut! Yet those with little oil or lack of His Spirit cried out, "Lord, Lord open to us!" But He answered them and said, "Assuredly, I say to you, I do not know you".

Jesus now gives a warning Verse 13

"Watch therefore, for you know neither the day nor the hour in which the Son of Man is coming"

In this truth depicted in picture form we see that all the ten virgins expected to enter the feast, the acid test was the "oil in the lamp" the oil is symbolic of the Holy Spirit.

As a child in Sunday School, we would sing a chorus:

"Give me oil in my lamp keep me burning, give me oil in my lamp I pray, keep me burning till the break of day"

What was that song saying?

If our light goes out, it's evidence that the oil is no longer present in our life.

The song is asking for the oil to be maintained until the dawn of either the day of His return or the day of our death - "keep me burning". This day of Judgment is self-determined, yet we have access to the Holy Spirit.

Jesus speaks of the Evil Tenants in the Vineyard (Luke 20:19) and there is a day of reckoning!

Jesus again tells a parable of Talents also found in Matthew 25.

The owner leaves his goods in the hands of three servants, according to their giftings and potential, he gives five, two and one talents.

The first two respond as they are committed to the Master and imbibe his philosophy and purpose.

The third one has no knowledge or perception of his heart and accuses him of being judgmental, uncaring and unreasonable.

Jesus speaks about this unjust servant having the little he had taken away from him and

"Cast the worthless servant into outer darkness, in that place there will be weeping and gnashing of teeth".

You may say, "where is the compassion in this?"

Yet the fact that five virgins understood and two out of the three servants understood defines the difference between the willingness of people to seek and secure truth rather than attempt to " freewheel " it into the kingdom of God by a door that is not open to us.

Jesus again speaks: "Enter through the narrow gate; for the gate is wide and the way is broad that leads to destruction, and there are many who enter through it. For the gate is small and the way is narrow that leads to life, and there are few who find it" (Matthew 7:13-14)

Jesus went through the towns and villages, teaching as he went, always pressing on toward Jerusalem. Someone asked him, "Lord, will only a few be saved?" He replied, "Work hard to enter the narrow door to God's Kingdom, for many will try to enter but will fail. When the master of the house has locked the door, it will be too late. You will stand outside knocking and pleading, 'Lord open the door for us!' But He will reply, 'I don't know you or where you come from.' Then you will say, 'But we ate and drank with, and You taught in our streets'. And He will reply, 'I tell you, I don't know you or where you come from. Get away from me, all you who do evil.'

"There will be weeping and gnashing of teeth..." (Luke 13:22-28 NLT)

This was a vivid description and answer to a simple question, 'Are there few who are saved?"

Having said this, the Judgment seat of God is also seen as the place of reward, the Judgment seat or 'Bema" seat often referred to by Bible scholars is also the seat that judged the athletic sports' events. It is there that the wreath was given to the winners.

Paul recognises the significance to the Christian; If the great white throne determines the sheep from the goats, then the Bema seat can be the place that determines the Christians performance in the race of life.

When are we to be judged and rewarded?

On "that Day" the day of The Lord.

Finally, there is laid up for me the crown of righteousness, which The Lord, the righteous judge, will give me on that Day, and not to me only but also to all who have loved His appearing.

(2 Timothy 4:8 NKJV)

so Christ was offered once to bear the sins of many. To those who eagerly wait for Him He will appear a second time, apart from sin, for salvation. (Hebrews 9:28 NKJV)

So, Paul is urging the Christian to live and expect the coming of The Lord. In these two scriptures, we see phrases such as "loved His appearing" and "eagerly wait for Him". It was a daily expectation, the early Christian fervently believed and therefore lived as if His coming was imminent.

Paul finishes his letter to the Corinthian Christians with the Aramaic "Maranatha" either "come Lord" or "The Lord comes" - this greeting also appeared in the Didache

The teachings of the twelve Apostles, "come Lord" can be seen as a call for the Second Advent to happen, "come Lord" can be seen as a creedal prayer.

This one phrase became a statement to so many Christian

Communities over the last two thousand years.

It is only the 21st Century leaders who have made a conscious decision to relinquish this substantial teaching from the theology of this generation.

Few sermons can now be heard, even among significant Church leaders.

Themes on living issues, life's conditions and the formula of prosperity may have shades of truth, yet the comprehensive teaching on accountability and judgment have been deliberately ignored under the heading of "not seeker-friendly" that is, to the Christian Church what political correctness is to the rest of the World, what is said is not actually wrong, but it might cause offence to some oversensitive person!

We are not speaking of any human teaching that must be accountable to the law of the land. We as citizens of this world should be extremely willing to lead the way on such issues as discrimination, be it social or spiritual.

However, the biblical truth of sin, righteousness and the judgment to come is the very reason that the Holy Spirit came.

He leads us into all truth. He must be able through the preaching, teaching and discipleship offered, to make provision for those three aspects of conviction to be clearly explained to a lost generation.

Think about it, He convicts the world of sin. When was the last time your friend, who attended your Church, came out convicted [not condemned] of sin?

He convicts of Righteousness; simply, the acceptable and correct way of living through the death, burial, resurrection, and ascension of Christ.

When was the last time in your Church that a person was convicted to embrace the righteousness of Christ?

He convicts of the judgment to come.

We are back to the subject! When was the last time you saw

a Christian or unbeliever in your Church convicted over the judgment to come?

Not many? Notice, I didn't say make decisions, I said become disciples!

So, why won't the church corporately preach and teach the doctrine of Second Advent when it is estimated as being mentioned three times more than the First Advent?

It may have a number of reasons:

[1] the varied interpretations and theological views on this subject.

[2] a fear of offending the "seeker" with the suggestion of accountability, judgement, and hell.

[3] the division among Christians over the place of Israel.

[4] the lack of understanding of Anti-Christ.

Over the last twenty-five years, the teaching on hell, Hades, separation, and the lake of fire has almost become obsolete. It seems as if the very teaching that brought people to Christ over centuries, has now been conveniently replaced with how to overcome social, relational, and financial issues. Yes, these are living issues, yet not as a replacement for the serious subject of our external consequences.

Hebrews 3: 7 – 19

This serious challenge as to faith, it's retention, and the consequences of falling away is not preached to the level of Hebrews 11. This passage is a warning to the reader [a] do not harden your heart as in the rebellion [b] testing the grace of God [c] they grow astray in their hearts [d] they shall not enter rest [e] take care, brothers, lest there be in any of you an evil, unbelieving heart, leading you to fall away from the living God... [f] for we have come to share Christ, if indeed we hold our original confidence form to the end.

We return to our original question, what is a Christian?

A decision maker, or a disciple maker?

Paul describes thus, as his farewell statement says, "I have run the race kept the faith. Fought the good fight". We obviously see a continuance of witness. We are told that as a prelude to the Second Advent, many will depart from the faith some giving heed to seducing doctrines [those that appeal to the sensual nature of the recipient].

Yet, we seldom hear this preached. We are in danger of preaching "another gospel".

Revelation the last book in the bible, the last chapter, the last verse is the Second Advent!

If the Church shows hesitation on preaching and teaching these subjects, it's not surprising that it's in crisis over human sexuality and same sex marriage.

1994 was the year l transferred from football to full-time ministry, spending a weekend at Methodist Training College in Derbyshire, with forty men.

During the worship, l felt myself, being sucked out of my body and standing in the presence of the Lord.

I received knowledge of the financial crash that would hit the Nation in August 2007, the first U.K. bank rush in 140 years!

It was also revealed that same sex marriage would become the major challenge to the Christian Church - it would result in many Churches and clergy either giving up their marriage licensing, or having it removed.

Even with this subject, scripture is being ignored; it's not phobic to disagree with humanistic philosophy, you can love people without supporting their lifestyle.

The bible clearly speaks on other forms of sexual activity, adultery, fornication, just as vital in the overview of biblical relationships.

As in the days of Noah shall it be at the coming of Christ, eating, drinking, marriage, giving and taking - basically eat drink and be merry for tomorrow we die!

It also referred to the cities of Sodom & Gomorrah as a sign of a society without faith.

Yet many Christians have become intimidated in preaching clear scriptural instructions.

Paul even describes the situation over same sex relationships. But, we are told these scriptures are culturally outdated, like slavery, we have moved on. Yet, biblical sexuality is not oppression of human independence, it's the basis of population increase - the capability to reproduce.

Under the UK marriage act, unless a marriage is consummated, it's considered annulled (unless you are same sex) why? It can't happen, so marriage has had to be rearranged to accommodate same sex union. This raises the question, if it cannot be consummated, there can never be any adultery! Because one holds to biblical truth, leaves no reason why we don't love those who live a different lifestyle.

To brand many Christians as "homophobic" is in itself provocative. To disagree is part of our human freedom, phobic suggests irrational fear. The additional offence of these two cities was the social abuse. They openly stated that they cared for the poor, however, even though they gave coins to the most disadvantaged, that should exchange them for food, many died with the money returning to the state. This was a social injustice, giving the appearance of providing, yet contradicting that with restrictions.

Many people would say that society mirrors these communities both in relationship and social inequalities.

Second Advent teaching makes reference to a new world order that brings independent thinking into alignment with governmental philosophy.

Who really knows what the mark of the Beast is? This seems the first generation that can now actually produce a mark on the right hand or forehead.

Revelations 13:16-17 & 14:9-10

No one can buy or sell without the mark or the name of the beast or the number of his name.

With animals being chipped, with current information suggesting that within the next five years all our personal details can be inserted within the back of the hand, this would replace the needs for plastic, passport, bank details, club membership, security passes. The Telegraph newspaper featured Swedish employees who have been implanted with a chip the size of a grain of rice, this enables them to open doors, operate printers, buy smoothies at the wave of a hand.

The injection has become so popular that workers at the company hold parties for those willing to get implanted!

The Daily Mail Science desk asks the question, "Would you let your boss implant you with a chip?" Belgian firm offers to turn staff into cyborgs to replace ID cards [15:05:08]. It is believed that 10,000 people worldwide already have such a chipped Radio Frequency identification [RFID].

Outside of biblical warnings of an anti-Christ intention you would welcome it as a fantastic advance in security and media advancement, yet, again, little or no teaching on such subjects.

This is serious; if a chip becomes our only means of transacting life, to refuse it is a premature death sentence - no food, no home, no clothes, no travel!

This teaching has been major over the centuries when it was impossible to imagine, now when it's totally doable no teaching or preaching about it... why?

We are nearer the coming of Christ more than ever, however, are we looking for His appearing?

I suggest not!

We have become hesitant in addressing any subject that might seem controversial or provocative. It leaves us in danger of becoming "lukewarm" which will leave us being spit from His mouth.

Yes, I've seen the extreme teaching of some, yet not the teaching of the balanced Holy Spirit inspired leaders. Many have become enriched by the sales of their books on positive lifestyles and pursuit of excellence.

The gospel that saved millions over the centuries has now been rebranded as a marketing skill to attract those who ideally would like to see Christianity as an additive rather than an alternative.

I love worship. I've been a worshipper all my Christian life, I appreciates many styles of worship, however, many songs today are created as album fillers

They lack depth of truth, doctrine, and are often performed rather than Holy Spirit inspired.

Take away the dark auditorium [sanctuary is out!] the flashing lights, smoke machines and distorted mixing and what are you left with?

Reading a recent worship report from the USA, it was saying that many contemporary Churches are losing young adults to Orthodox and traditional liturgical Churches.

When the survey asked why, the majority said, "we came out of that world of night clubs, we want something that has been stable for many years, something distinctively different".

What are we saying?

Not all preaching or worship is compromised, no, much is evidenced by the Holy Spirit, what we are saying is that many of the "Jesus Doctrines" are fading from our preaching, teaching, and worship.

When He comes, will he find faith on the earth? (Luke 18: 8)

So, a major part of the "doctrines of Jesus" are either missing or transparent from the normality of Church teaching.

What we have replaced them with is verging on a "different gospel" which is emerging from a "different spirit" leading to a "different Jesus"

For if he who comes preaches another Jesus whom we have not preached, or if you receive a different spirit which you have not received, or a different gospel which you have not accepted—you may well put up with it! (2 Corinthians 11:4 NKJV)

THE BLOOD OF CHRIST

We have briefly looked at the Communion and seen the differing theological views on the configuration of the emblems.

This is not a revisiting of the substance of this office rather a faith that is imbibed by blood. Christianity is blood inspired and blood redeeming.

Knowing that you were not redeemed with corruptible things like silver or gold from your aimless conduct received by tradition from your fathers, but with the precious blood of Christ as of a lamb without blemish and without spot. (1 Peter 1:18-19 NKJV)

The blood of Christ was efficacious in the transforming of the human heart in relationship with Almighty God. His death on Calvary made available the opportunity for repentant humanity to regain the tranquility of 'peace with God".

His blood was shed for the remission of sin - the cleaning of sin - to be at peace with God our redemption being brought back from afar. Our guilt being blotted out, purges our conscience, became His own peculiar possession. It makes us priests and kings unto God, we are justified, sanctified. We have eternal security, made one in Christ, we are reconciled with Christ and the Father. We can enter the holy of holies, we have a fellowship with God, we are made one, we have an eternal inheritance. We have overcome the Devil.

The Christian faith is a "blood faith" from the beginning of time, the sacrifice of something innocent was offered for the perpetrator.

This concept of the innocent for the guilty is seen as far back as Genesis 3:2. God provides the clothing to cover Adam and Eve's nakedness.

From that time, offerings of animals were commonplace.

Even with Cain and Abel, a lamb was the offering acceptable to God. This had been clearly explained by the example of God's provision for their parents during the expulsion from Eden.

Cain was even given a second chance, "If you do well, will you not be accepted? And if you do not do well sin lies at the door" (Genesis 4:7 NKJV)

For the life of the flesh is in the blood and I have given it to you on the altar to make atonement for your souls; for it is the blood that makes atonement for the soul. (Leviticus 17:11 NKJV)

Even in the primitive days of the old testament, the realisation of life being maintained through blood was revealing.

The old covenant was seen as animals without any blemish being sacrificed by the priest as the atoning, forgiving process; one hand on the person, the other on the head of the lamb or designated animal showing the transfer of the person's sin to the innocent animal.

Once a year, the high priest washed and clothed in his priestly robes would take some blood of the guilt offering and the priest shall put it on the lobe of the right ear of the one to be cleansed and on the thumb of his right hand and on his big toe of his right foot. (Leviticus 14:4)

This ritual was symbolic of the Christ to come who as John Baptist declared, "Behold the Lamb of God who takes away the sin of the world." (John 1:29 NKJV)

This is a foretaste of Christ who became the High Priest after the order of Melchizedek, however it was His own blood that smeared his body and was poured out on the cross of Calvary, this was his Mercy Seat.

By no longer preaching a 'blood' gospel, many preachers have reduced the message to one of human logic rather than divine provision.

To preach a blood inspired gospel is offensive to the intellectual humanistic philosophy, even barbaric to some.

In a genuine attempt by some to explain the benefits of salvation, they have omitted the very method of entry into this salvation.

A bloodless faith excuses the need for a Cross, so it leads to a 'cross-less' gospel.

Paul however maintains the message, "I preach Christ and Him crucified"

It is still the power [dunamis] of our salvation; I plead with preachers reading this book and members of Churches to challenge and to be challenged to 'preach Christ and Him crucified" -forget the offence it will bring to the religious or the embarrassment to the intellectual, it remains the only method of truth and lasting transformation.

Life is maintained in the blood, many religions see the need of sacrifice through blood, yet they have missed the sacrifice laid down for us before the foundation of the world.

You can see a pattern from the Old to the New Testament emerging, the blood of the temporal was contaminated by the sinful actions of the first Adam, the last Adam (Christ) being God made flesh, justified many by the shedding of the blood, His own blood, that of the Son of God, yet also the son of man. The eternal blood covenant made precious by the death and resurrection of Jesus. He who saved us from our sins, did it for us. Amen!

The Salvation Army regarded the 'blood' as integral to the gospel message as mentioned earlier in the book, 'blood & fire" have been the watchwords of this Christian worldwide agency.

The ancient writers of the Old Testament understood before scientific proof that there was life in the blood.

It's the blood that often reveals the health or sickness of the human frame.

Hebrews commenting on the old covenant says, "Almost all things are by the law purged with blood and without the shedding of blood is no remission". (Hebrews 9:22 KJV)

The blood makes "atonement" basically to cover, to hide, to shelter.

So, the call to the churches is "don't devalue the blood of Christ by not preaching or teaching about it"! In the spiritual as well as the natural there is life in the blood.

For two thousand years, the Christian Church has weathered changes in doctrine, style and even persecution, however, it has not jettisoned the doctrine of the blood of Christ. If we do, on the basis that this society would not appreciate its language, we preach another gospel which will be anathema to God.

General William Booth, founder of the Salvation Army said:

"The chief dangers which confront the coming century will be religion without the Holy Ghost, Christianity without Christ, forgiveness without repentance, Salvation without regeneration, politics without God and heaven without hell." (Funk & Wagnalls 1902 Homilectic Review Volume 44)

He could have been describing the beginning of the 21st century. We often marginalise the power of the Holy Spirit, substituting it for the power of the media! The message of forgiveness has little element of repentance in today's society.

It is often the case that Christians will justify blatant sin by applying "I'm forgiven by His Grace" there is however little if any true repentance or even victory over temptation.

Many today would identify themselves as Christians, yet there is little or no regeneration evidence - governmental decisions show a distinct absence of Christian values.

Both heaven and especially hell are' no go' areas for many preachers.

So, we see the evidence before our eyes of a society that has influenced the Church rather than the other way round.

The two greatest blood covenants as seen in the bible are the Passover and the Passover meal hosted by Christ.

The Children of Israel had become slaves to the Egyptian nation, their prayers had come up before Almighty God.

After the plagues had not resulted in freedom, God brought freedom through the blood of the lamb.

The Jews painted the blood of a lamb over the door lintel; the command was 'stay under the blood' as the angel of death visited Egypt that night. The promise was simple yet profound, 'When I see the blood I will pass over you".

The way to avoid death of the first born had conditions.

[1] They had to apply the blood. Good deeds and attendance to the temple would not qualify them. it was the blood that covered any sin or failure.

[2] They had to stay under the blood - the house that had the covering for the people. If they left the house they would have died.

The Passover meal – Communion - the conditions remain the same.

This time for the world, not just the Jewish nation.

[1] We need to apply the blood. This time not to our house made with hands but to our lives. It's the blood of Christ that cleanses us from all unrighteousness. As we submit to his request, He covers us with His sacrifice, "The Lamb of God who takes away the sin of the world".

[2] We need to stay under the blood.

Paul mentions those who have gone out from among us as they were not of us."Some will depart from the faith giving heed to seducing doctrines of demons. You ran well but who hindered you?"

As we near death, when the angel of death draws near to the soul of man, it's only the blood of Christ that can make him 'pass over'.

So, we are a blood faith, not ashamed to testify the fact that we have been transfused by his blood, translated by his word and transformed by his spirit.

FAITH

So, faith comes from hearing and hearing through the word of Christ. (Romans 10:17 ESV)

Faith is not a self-generated belief, it is conceived by the Holy Spirit through preaching and reading the Word.

A Definition of Faith is belief, trust and loyalty. It is to persuade, it implies such knowledge of, assent to, and confidence in certain divine truths, especially those of the gospel.

The old testament Hebrew language develops the word faith to include the individual feeling of safety, to feel secure and to acknowledge a dependency on God for protection.

In the Synoptic gospels, faith is confident trust based on God's promise and understood through His word. Faith is not a mystical acquisition gained by the mystic Celts of old, even though they undoubtedly moved in breathtaking faith. It isn't a gift only to those of monastic calling. It's a basic element of the Christian experience. Without faith, it's impossible to please God. Hebrews 11: 6.

We are saved by God's grace through faith, then it's a gift, it's not ourselves. Faith & grace are gifts of God. Faith is gifted to humanity so that they can respond to and connect with the Almighty.

Paul recognises that we, as Christians, walk by faith and not by sight. In simple terms, faith is not generated by human understanding on Christ.

Sadly, in some sections of the Christian Church, we see people either obsessed with faith, or through an extreme Calvinistic theology, little need to mature in it!

To some faith has a formula and it becomes an elixir for all ills; a belief that faith dictates destiny. Faith however, rather than dictating our future, equips us to overcome regardless of the future.

The Amplified Bible (AMP) begins Hebrews 11 with:

Now faith is the assurance (title deed, confirmation) of things (we) hope for, being proof of things (we do not see) and the conviction of their reality (faith perceiving as real fact what is not revealed to the senses).

Faith is not advanced belief. Belief is based generally on endorsement, personal experience or referral from trusted people enabling one to have confidence in a person or opportunity.

Faith however is not belief based on human logic or human expectation, it is a superhuman ability to expect what others see as impossible. It is God's belief infused into the human heart.

All things become possible to those who believe with the additive of faith!

Faith 'Pistis' speaks of persuasion, credence, moral conviction of religious truth. Faith undoubtedly brings conviction of a certainty, "I know who I have believed and am persuaded that he is able to keep that which I have committed unto Him." (2 Timothy 1:12)

True faith purifies our motives; it is based on the will of Christ, rather than the pleasure and intent of man.

Faith enables fallen man to engage with the risen Christ, faith stretches across the grave of certainty and offers a resurrection into the guarantees of the atonement.

Faith retains buoyancy in the midst of the most dramatic storm.

Faith is listed alongside hope and love as the most stoic of the attributes that God infuses into the heart of every believer. However, faith as we know it will be completed when we stand before Him!

When we are truly seated with Christ in heavenly places, our faith will be exchanged for sight, we will see Him as He is, and we will be like Him!

Hope will also be completed, all the expectancy bubbling up within the heart of the believer will become reality – seen and lived in.

Love, however, will be the central force for eternity - God is love. God so loved the world that He gave His only begotten son (John 3:16) that Agape love may transcend and transform human love for each other.

Faith is the connecting cord that links the heart of the Almighty to the believer.

Faith links time with eternity, it is eternal in origin, yet manifested on earth by those who seek and wish to maintain their relationship with Almighty God.

Faith sees things as they should be, could be, or will be.

[1] **Should be:**

Faith completes or corrects as needed to fulfill destined outcomes; when we see what should be happening, and we surrender to the purpose of God, then the outcomes are realised.

[2] **Could be:**

Faith sees the potential of the next stage of our destiny not yet developed yet possible in Christ Jesus.

[3] Will be:

Faith sees no reason for the lack of completion – it only sees the finished product... it sees it as if it already is!

In biblical terms, faith sees a land flowing with milk and honey when reality only sees the wilderness!

When logic overrides faith, an eleven-day journey turns into a forty-year saga for the children of Israel!

Faith provided clothes, food and shoes that remained throughout the journey; logic defeated all that generation - they never entered the promised land apart from families of Joshua and Caleb. Logic was based on fear, faith brought courage.

When Joshua was inducted into the leadership of the people after the departure of Moses, both God and the people called for him to "be of good courage" basically, 'Have Faith"!

Faith is not needed if practical solutions are readily available, I hear some Christians saying - "I'm living by faith, brother!"

What some mean is "I'm not willing to work for my bread!" Unless there is a God given reason for not working like Paul did to support himself, then the scripture comes into force, "Man shall work by the sweat of his brow".

Faith has a lookalike - its name? Presumption! It appears through deception, it is misquoting the scriptures. taking them out of context and presenting them as precepts. I hear people exulting from the platform saying, "remind God of His promises" I say, don't bother! He never forgets!

Faith never makes you feel inadequate, that you are to blame for someone's death, sickness. If the preacher has faith, ask him to do the miracle!

Faith is a basic ingredient in the Christian lifestyle, Jesus said that just one grain of it can remove your mountain of opposition

Belief is the brother of faith, belief engages faith and faith causes us to believe!

Faith is the spiritual infusion into the belief of the human spirit. Belief is when we, through our own will, have the confidence in the promises of God.

Unbelief is belief that has not risen yet to the level needed to confidently submit to the impossibility of human logic.

Disbelief however is the discontinuance of belief; it is the severing of the cord of confidence in the reality of His word.

So, faith is engaged with the spirit of man, belief with his soul and cognitive abilities.

Faith is a discipline not a feeling.

14

FASTING

The state of going without food or drink – voluntarily – generally for religious purposes.

Nelson's dictionary

Often in the Old Testament, the people fasted when facing crisis, or when mourning loss.

Then the Lord said to Moses, "Write these words, for according to the tenor of these words I have made a covenant with you and with Israel." (Exodus 34:27 NKJV)

We see here a different form of fasting, normally fasting had been associated with distress, opposition, frustration, fear. Moses is engaged with God in conversation, he is about to receive a revelation that will declare the purposes of God; the requirements needed for a fallen world to be reconciled to Himself. This was not to get something, it was to become something. It wasn't a crisis, but a chrysalis. Moses had fasted for forty days, preparing him for the law of God to be revealed. Moses experiences a transforming moment during the forty-day self-motivated fast.

This was new for Moses; the only corporate directional fast was the Day of Atonement. And remember, neither was this a crisis! It was a prophetic symbol of the Christ to come, sins forgiven and freedom from the constraints of failure or condemnation. Therefore, fasting was not an outlet for dealing with crisis, but rather a celebration of the solution.

As we come to the New Testament, Mark 9:29 (NKJV) gives us an interesting view on the power of fasting. Jesus sees the crowd, the scribes and the disciples arguing. On drawing near he asks the question, "What are you arguing about with them?

A voice in the crowd replies:

"Teacher, I brought my son to you for he has a spirit that makes him mute". He continues, "I asked your disciples to cast it out, but they were not able"

Jesus reacts to this news by addressing the disciples, "O faithless generation, how long am I to be with you?"

After this, He released the boy immediately. In private, the disciples - who had often healed the sick and cast out demons - asked the question, "why could we not cast it out?"

The reply was that, "this kind come out by prayer and fasting"

This statement triggered something within my spirit. We started this subject by saying that in the Old Testament many fasted when in danger, trouble or need. However, Moses showed us that he fasted not to get but to become! The Day of Atonement was effectively a celebration not of the problem of sin being dealt with, but that humanity could become righteous!

With Moses and with Jesus they fasted before the event - Moses to receive the Law and Jesus to uphold Grace. We tend to fast to seek something - either breakthrough or break out.

The story of Jesus, I believe, answers a lot of questions about new covenant fasting. Jesus did not say that fasting would end on the day of Pentecost. He had breathed on them, anointing them with the spirit so that they had authority to do the commands of the Lord, so why couldn't they release this boy?

Come back to me with the baptism of Jesus.

In Matthew 3:13 – 4:1-7 I believe that there are key factors that could revolutionise your thinking on fasting.

1.   Jesus was obedient in being baptised even though He apparently didn't need it. What was His reason? "It is fitting to fulfill all righteousness". Baptism is the symbolism of being buried with Him; He died for our penalty of sin. He was laid in the tomb as a man must be, yet the grave could not hold its prey – up from the grave he arose!

Note "To fulfill all righteousness" we are told that the effectual fervent prayer of a righteous man makes tremendous power available James 5:16 (AMP). So, the question is, if baptism if fulfilling all righteousness – have you been baptised since surrendering your life to Christ? This is the first stage towards Christ's fasting.

Baptism comes after confession not before; burial is after death and before resurrection. Baptism is an integral part of the salvation process. "Repent and be baptized every one of you in the name of Jesus Christ for the remission of sins." (Acts 2:38 KJV)

Baptism is not just symbolic, it is obedience to the process of redemption. We are not baptised to be saved but it is, however, part of a salvation process in the life of the believer. The thief on the Cross, like others to come, could not enter the waters of baptism, but still entered into the paradise of the Father. After death to the old life there needs to be a funeral, a laying in the ground of the past, publicly. I once had a deaf lady rise from the waters with her hearing restored!

2.   The heavens opened and the Holy Spirit descended. Christians need to experience both the 'open heaven' of God and

be 'empowered of the Holy Spirit'. This is vital if we are to engage in a new fast - repent, be baptised, and you shall receive the Holy Spirit. As Jesus stood in the waters, the Holy Spirit descended with the symbolic purity of a dove. It was the peace, and new beginning that entered the righteous frame of the Son of Man. It's the very same Sprit that empowers us.

But if the spirit of Him who raised Jesus from the dead dwells in you, He who raised Christ Jesus from the dead will also give life to your mortal bodies through His Sprit who dwells in you. (Romans 8:11 NASB)

Acts 2 was not for a temporal Apostolic age now spent in the pages of history. His mandate is still to convict the world of Sin, Righteousness and the Judgement to come. He came to dwell in and on every believer, enabling them to become; and to fashion disciples of every nation, healing the sick, raising the dead, delivering the bound. The Holy Spirit, the third person of the Divine trilogy, is resident upon this planet until the imminent return of the Christ. Then as He removes Himself, the Christ will return in the like manor that His disciples saw Him go.

3.   Then Jesus was led up by the Spirit into the wilderness to be tempted. Never enter the wilderness unless you are both filled with and led by the Holy Spirit! The wilderness is not the place for any believer unless instructed by the Spirit of God. If we are to fast, then it is vital for us to be led by the Holy Spirit. Those who are being led by the Spirit of God, these are the sons of God (Romans 8:14).

There is authority in the name of Jesus especially to those who obey and hear what the Spirit is saying to the Church.

4.   And when he had fasted forty days and forty nights, afterward He was hungry (Matthew 4:2 NKJV). Note that the

temptation of Christ took place AFTER the forty day fast, when Jesus was hungry. Now when the tempter came... the fast was not a reaction to temptation, it was a preparation for the temptation. Fasting therefore is not to get something or to remove something, it is to BE something.

5.   The temptation came against Jesus in three aspects of one's life...

a.   Provision: He was hungry. He was tempted to change the stones into bread. We are often tempted to channel our spirituality into the temporal things that we seem to need for daily living. The need was genuine, the means of supplying it was not. We can easily be side-tracked in the pursuit and application of the basics of life. Some decades ago, when I had just started in the insurance industry, I had promised to speak at a youth camp for recovering drug addicts. But I was also desperate for finance to live! I was tempted by a fantastic opportunity to travel to Stoke on Trent for enough business to keep me in 'bread' for months. But I turned it down to keep my word.

The result of not submitting to temptation? A miracle! Two weeks later I met that unknown future client in the middle of Birmingham, and we conducted the business anyway. I was reminded that He never sees the righteous begging bread.

b.   Presumption: He was tempted to act on a misquoted scripture. Are we ever tempted to interpret a 'now word' that seems to suit the situation at hand, yet it is a perversion of its meaning? Basically, we have taken it out of context! I have received many 'words from God" from genuine people, however the contents had no consistency with the message I was hearing personally from the Lord. You can, even in all innocence, misquote scripture or take it out of context - a proof text must never be taken out of context!

c.   Position: He was offered something He already had. Jesus actually said, "whoever wants to be a leader among you must be your servant" (Mark 10:43). Few actually require no badge or title to distinguish them from the rest of the crowd. My friend Dave Cooper, Canon to the Ordinary for OSL worked, in his former life, in the music business. He told me the story of those seeking the 'AAA' pass – the coveted backstage 'Access All Areas' badge that every fan or crew member would want to wear. But he said there was a greater level of authority – to achieve such status that no pass was required. When you could 'access all areas' without the badge, just a nod to security as they waved you by, as he could, then this was the mark of true authority. The world recognises that there is something greater than a badge. There is the inner authority that requires no mark. The mother of two brothers who followed Jesus wanted to know if they could sit at His right hand and left hand in the kingdom to come. Yet Jesus said, "Only my Father knows these things".

6.   Behold, Angels came and ministered to him. It was then that miracles began to manifest; it was His victory over temptation that pre-meditated the angelic vision.

What are we saying then on fasting?

The disciples had not understood fasting. They saw it as a reactionary event when needed, a 'bondage breaker'. It was, however, obvious that Jesus was teaching a new perception of fasting. Fasting is not necessarily to attempt to negate the problem, it is to build you up to deal with the problem! Jesus was tempted after the forty day fast. It may have left him physically weaker, however He was spiritually stronger – more than capable of overcoming the temptations set before him.

So, when you fast, see it as a faith-building exercise. It is not to remove a wall of opposition or to shrink it, it is to help you grow bigger than any problem you have not yet encountered.

THE GROWTH PATTERN OF A CHRISTIAN

Therefore, having been justified by faith, we have peace with God through our Lord Jesus Christ, through whom also we have access by faith into this grace in which we stand, and rejoice in hope of the glory of God. (Romans 5:1-2 NKJV)

We are told to identify Christians by their fruit - this is safer than by their gift. Yet what is the process of becoming a Christian and the spiritual journey we must take?

Paul, speaking of the overcoming Christian as one who progresses through a divine process, says it is a growth pattern that enables them to live not a perfect life, but one of victory and stability.

Paul sees faith as the ingredient that brings justification, which leads to peace with God. Faith actually unlocks the door of Grace, this bringing Justification, leading to Peace with God. One is then found rejoicing and living in Hope; hope releases the glory of God that is available to all.

Paul says that we have been justified in simple terms. It's as if someone looks at our record of life and it looks 'just as if I had never sinned!' The guilt of our trespasses and the files of our spiritual misdemeanors have been expunged. When there is a spiritual check against our character, we are faultless, though we are not guiltless!

All of this is obtained by faith. That implants into the heart of every person who truly asks Christ to intervene in the daily workings of their being.

Let me say that again. Faith is the belief of God implanted into the heart of every person who truly asks Christ to intervene in daily workings of their life.

This faith, obtained through Christ, so brings peace between a sinful man and a Holy God! Faith is the heartbeat of life in Christ; it's the pacemaker that maintains the heart throb of eternal life.

We have access to faith! This releases his grace so that one can be justified through that Faith so releasing his peace; this alone generates rejoicing, the spontaneous outbreak of adoration. The reconciliation of fallen man with a risen Christ!

To all believers, the magnitude of His glory is revealed.

Peace with God brings the Peace of God. When Jesus left this world, He left his peace. "Peace I leave with you, My peace I give to you; not as the world gives do I give to you." (John 14:27 NKJV).

Yet, grace is coming!

through whom also we have access by faith into this grace in which we stand, and rejoice in the Hope of the Glory of God. (Romans 5:2 NKJV)

In simple English – FAITH (God's super belief) enables us to become JUSTIFIED (just as if I had never sinned) through Grace (God's favour).

So, as Christians we enjoy special treatment; not because of our own righteousness, but because he is righteous.

Let's break that down a bit.

Paul is saying that a Christian now has credibility before God justified not through good deeds, or actions of kindness, or by human effort, but through faith (God's super belief) and that comes by hearing the word of God.

Romans 10:17 tells us that this faith becomes available after hearing the dynamics of the preached word. This faith brings peace beyond human understanding; it turns the key in the door of grace (God's favour) which enables us to experience the things of God that we would never have expected!

So, as you read this now, faith can seep into you, opening the door of Grace.

When we understand the magnitude of his Love for us, we then rejoice in hope, we now have expectations, direction for the future, a purpose for living and an assurance in dying.

Paraphrasing Paul, he is saying that before you became a Christian, you had little or no access to the knowledge of God, yet one day, the word of God convicted you of sin, righteousness and the judgment to come by the Holy Spirit – it made us aware of our condition, spiritually, before God.

Knowing that there is a God-shaped void in our life, the Holy Spirit again showed us that we could become righteous (doing and thinking the way God always intended us to). We now have to make a decision: do we continue in sin (self) or accept this gift of faith? By accepting this gift of faith and experiencing His grace we are led to become justified (just as if I had not sinned). This then causes us to rejoice in hope of His glory (his abundance and prosperity).

The Glory of God is both who He is and the abundance of His provision. He is magnified in all His ways, He is outstanding in His countenance, He prospers the soul of mankind, He is limitless in His dealings with the human soul.

Notice the progress of our faith:

FAITH – GRACE – JUSTIFICATION – PEACE – REJOICING – GLORY OF GOD

These are the ingredients of salvation; every believer experiences this divine process. Moses wanted to see his glory; Moses wanted to see the magnitude of His power and personality.

Moses asked to, 'See His Glory' however due to the Holiness of God, no human could ever see his face. But the Almighty nonetheless made provision. Moses stood on, and was covered by, a rock. This was symbolic; prophetically introducing Christ the Rock who would one day become the covering for humanity in its quest to "see His glory" Exodus 33.

Moses also made a request that humanity still asks today, 'show me the way' followed by the question, 'who will go with me?' This is still the cry of many today.

We, as mortal creatures, who have but fleeting breath inside, that for whom this journey of life is but a shaft of light in the great expanse of eternity – we all need to shout to the heavens:

'Show us the way!'

For Moses, it was to hide himself in the 'Rock of Christ'. Jesus openly answers that question to us today, "I am the Way, the Truth and the Life, no man comes to the Father except through Me" (John 14:6 NKJV)

Moses understood his dependency on the presence of God and proclaimed, "If Your presence does not go with me, I'm not going."

As a pastor for five decades, I can say with certainty that this statement is true. What is the point of us reaching out for temporal gratification if it does not lead to eternal satisfaction?

Moses knew this. He needed to see the glory of the Lord.

Simeon, holding the child Jesus in his hands, said, "let Your servant depart in peace for my eyes have seen the glory of the Lord in the land of the living."

To see the prosperity of the Lord is the completion of our journey on earth. When we, like Moses, receive answers to such sincere requests, we receive a revelation of His glory.

Moses was promised the following:

"My goodness will pass before you"

We are surrounded by His goodness. David said, "Surely goodness and mercy shall follow me all the days of my life"

"I will proclaim the name of the Lord before you"

The name of the Lord is a strong tower. There is strength in the proclamation of His name.

"I will be gracious to whom I will be gracious"

The favour of God is not based on merit but on His generosity.

"I will have compassion on whom I will have compassion".

The whole Christian faith is based on the compassion of Christ. Compassion is the expression of sensitivity, gentleness, care, concern, mercy and kindness to those who suffer.

He took upon Himself the guilt, pain, sin, sickness and rejection of a fallen humanity.

It was of the future Christ that Father God said to Moses

"Here is a place by Me and you will stand on the rock"

It was this reality that inspired Rev'd Augustus Montague Toplady (1740-1778) to pen the famous hymn, Rock of Ages.

Caught in a storm while walking the gorge at Burrington Combe in the Mendip Hills, England, Toplady found shelter in a gap in the rock.

When I draw this fleeting breath,

When mine eyes shall draw close in death

When I soar to worlds unknown

See Thee on thy judgment throne

Rock of ages cleft for me

Let me hide myself in thee.

It is the closeness with the rock that enables us to see His Glory. When we see that glory, we are translated by knowledge into eternal time. While the earth dims, Heaven shines.

Every believer has this promise of everlasting life. Simeon having seen the Glory of the lord in the form of the child Jesus Christ calls out "Let your servant depart in peace".

Why? Because he had glimpsed – no – he had handled eternal life made flesh and now dwelling with man, as a man!

It is little wonder, then, that Apostle Paul continues to say, "we also glory in tribulations, knowing that tribulation produces perseverance".

We know that a Christian has the out-workings of the attributes previously mentioned. We know what a Christian is, and the characteristics manifested in the process. Once we have understood this process, at work within every believer, we can then engage in the next process that reveals the maturity needed for our spiritual growth as Christians.

We must not imagine that 'committing our life to Christ' is the end of the process of salvation. It is truly the beginning of the stages of maturity.

"And I, brethren, could not speak to you as to spiritual people but as to carnal, as to babes in Christ. I fed you with milk and not with solid food; for until now you were not able to receive it, and even now you are still not able; for you are still carnal. For where there are envy, strife, and divisions among you, are you not carnal and behaving like mere men? For when one says, "I am of Paul," and another, "I am of Apollos," are you not carnal? Who then is Paul, and who is Apollos, but ministers through whom you believed, as the Lord gave to each one? I planted, Apollos watered, but God gave the increase. So then neither he who plants is anything, nor he who waters, but God who gives the increase. (1 Corinthians 3:1-7 NKJV)

Paul is identifying the difference between spiritual people and carnal people, allegorically comparing carnal natures as babies in Christ – unable to yet receive meat but being fed with milk. Maturity – moving beyond envy, strife and disunity - renders the ability within the believer to receive the word of righteousness and to learn the oracles of God. Hebrews 5:12-13

So, as Christians, we need to understand the reality of our faith, rather than any illusory construct, that would be compared with the imagination of children. Because this is no fairy story, crafted and stylised with tall tales and happily ever after for all. There is a requirement, a choice and a commitment; available to all, but not accepted by all.

Once we have grasped this concept of our faith, Paul then exalts the power of this progression of our Christian life:

"We also glory in Tribulations" – the anguish, burden, persecution and troubles of this world. This produces patience, perseverance, endurance and continuance, which develops character, experience and trustworthiness - which produces hope, joyful anticipation and expectation.

And with hope, we are not disappointed, Paul assures us, "because the love of God has been poured out in our hearts by the Holy Spirit who was given to us." (Romans 5:5 NKJV)

Hope is reinforced by the Love of God!

Paul is not in any way advocating a life of pain and disadvantage.

He is acknowledging, however, that Christians may often travel a road of persecution. The Christian lifestyle isn't as slick and trendy as the modern 'media' style churches may seek to suggest: it's not a 'blast', it's more likely to be eruptive! Truth is challenging. Truth does not adapt to the whim of the people. Truth has the capacity to confront and stand its ground, with the immoveable conviction of righteousness. And yet, moving, as Paul describes, beyond a carnal relationship with the world, truth becomes something more. It is a comfort, the structure, the promise and the constant; indeed, it is the Rock upon which our faith is founded.

To mitigate the persecution and trials of our faith, to dilute our truth, is to preach 'another gospel'. History is littered with the blood of the martyr. The early church and the imploding church of history have the same DNA and manifestations.

Paul is saying that, rather than deterring us from the faith, tribulation produces a desire to persevere; to maintain our calling. There is a freedom in the Spirit coupled with a testing of one's faith.

So, these testing circumstances are used by the Lord to grow us in faith and determination. A 'painless gospel' is a western culture, rather than a theological certainty. The 'prosperity gospel', in its extreme, gives no credence to biblical and world history.

Throughout our lives and ministry, we will experience hard times; be it as a Christian, as churches or as families. However, it is our response, our reaction to these situations, that depicts the theology we embrace.

I have, at times, as a pastor wanted to 'cut and run'. I'm sure many in ministry can relate to this. However, when Peter was asked by Jesus, "will you also leave Me?" the reply came back, "You are the only one with the words of eternal life" and that's the bottom line! No, I will not give up. I'm here for the journey.

"I have found the paradox that if you love until it hurts, there can be no more hurt, only more love" Mother Teresa

What a thought. Just love; love beyond, love until there is no longer any element of hurt left within us.

If we didn't face trials, how would we exercise our faith?

"Trials teach us what we are, they dig up the soil and let us see what we are made of."

Charles Haddon Spurgeon

True Christian faith is more than belief; it's the security of our eternal future this side of the grave. The testing of our faith speaks more to our pending success rather than our pending loss.

We are more than conquerors through Christ who strengthens us.

If people have the courage to die for him every day, shouldn't we have the courage to live for Him every day?